The Art of Tying The Wet Fly & Fishing The Flymph

James E. Leisenring

The Art of Tying The Wet Fly

&

Fishing The Flymph

JAMES E. LEISENRING

VERNON S. HIDY

New Introduction by ERNEST SCHWIEBERT

CROWN PUBLISHERS, INC., NEW YORK

LIBRARY OF CONGRESS CATALOG CARD NUMBER 71-147319
PRINTED IN THE UNITED STATES OF AMERICA
PUBLISHED SIMULTANEOUSLY IN CANADA
BY GENERAL PUBLISHING COMPANY LIMITED

Fifth Printing, November, 1977

"Pleasure is spread through the earth
In stray gifts to be claimed by whoever shall find."
—William Wordsworth

"The skill of technique is more than honesty; it is something wider, embracing honesty and grace and rule in an elevated and clear sentiment. It is made up of accumulated tradition, kept alive by individual pride, rendered exact by professional opinion, and, like the higher arts, it is spurred on and sustained by discriminating praise.

"This is why the attainment of proficiency, the pushing of your skill with attention to the most delicate shades of excellence, is a matter of vital concern. Efficiency of a practically flawless kind may be reached naturally in the struggle for bread. But there is something beyond, a subtle and unmistakable touch of love and pride beyond mere skill; almost an inspiration which gives to all work that finish which is almost art —which *is* art."

—Joseph Conrad

"Fly Fishing is a fair contest between the fish and the man. Success depends solely upon the caprice of the fish, your own skill and perseverance. That is much."
—Sidney Buxton

CONTENTS

EDITOR'S NOTE

BOOKS, PARTICULARLY FINE FISHING BOOKS, have a life and pertinence all their own: not only do they grow "on" and "in" a reader, but at times they also grow themselves. Such is the case here. The original edition of *The Art of Tying the Wet Fly,* published thirty years ago, was "told to" Vernon S. Hidy by the late "Wet-fly wizard of the Brodheads," James Leisenring. Though "Big Jim" has since died, his ideas and concepts on wet-fly fishing and tying certainly have not; through Pete Hidy, who often fished with Leisenring, they have continued to grow. It is thus an honor to reprint a fine old angling classic with some updating and with an exciting new section on the important "flymph fishing" concept; with a new appreciation by Ernest Schwiebert; and with a full dual attribution to both authors that has more than been earned.

N. L.

FOREWORD TO THE 1971 EDITION

THE IDEAS, ATTITUDES, AND TECHNIQUES of my friend Jim Leisenring have served me well as a guide to the pleasures of fly fishing for thirty-six years. I am delighted to see this new edition made available for new generations of anglers. When my editor, Nick Lyons, talked to me about adding some text of my own to the book I readily agreed to his suggestion. As one of the younger generation exposed to the continuing disproportionate emphasis on the "all-purpose" technique of the dry fly, Nick welcomed the idea of supplementing Leisenring's earlier book with my more recent observations.

"The Art of Fishing the Flymph" is nothing more, really, than an extension of Leisenring's Chapter 12, "Fishing the Wet Fly," in which he devoted barely five paragraphs to his method of "making a fly become deadly." He had planned to write, later, a book on this subject but time did not permit. Consequently, I wrote a series of three articles for *Sports Illustrated* on the broad subject of wet-fly fishing. This was published in book form in 1961 and is now available in the *Sports Illustrated* Library of Sport with full credit to Leisenring as the wet-fly genius who passed along many of his time-tested and trout-tested ideas to me.

After the articles and the book were published, I received many inquiries. These, plus my discussions with friends in the Flyfisher's Club of Oregon and the Federation of Fly Fishermen, revealed an important fact: all novices and many experienced fly fishermen have virtually no understanding of the drama of the aquatic insects struggling in view of the trout just beneath the surface of the water.

Since there is some ambiguity, confusion, and prejudice associated with the words "wet fly," "nymph fishing," "emerging nymphs," and "hatching insects," I coined the words "flymph" and "flymph fishing" in 1963. These words have been accepted by fly fishermen of my acquaintance who have found them useful. They accurately identify that dramatic and little-understood interval of an aquatic insect's life: the struggle up to the surface as well as the drift (of some insects) in or just below the surface film.

The techniques described in these pages are applicable to all species of trout, particularly the more discriminating brown trout and rainbow trout, which are noted for their selectivity in feeding. I trust the reader will find that my clarification of an old fishing technique, and my new terminology, will add to his fishing pleasure year after year on many streams and lakes.

VERNON S. HIDY

On the Fly Water,
Silver Creek, Idaho
10 October 1970

Vernon S. "Pete" Hidy

Some of the fascinating books recommended for the education of those who seek to improve their techniques and understanding of fly fishing.

INTRODUCTION
TO THE 1971 EDITION

Skues and Leisenring, side by side

THE WET-FLY WIZARD
OF THE BRODHEADS

IT WAS JOHN WALLER HILLS in his *History of Fly Fishing* who first outlined the cycles of innovation and discipledom present in angling literature. His perspective of fly-fishing history has an interesting corollary. Great fishermen are often shaped by the character of their rivers, and particular problems of tactics and fly dressing, but it is also true that the innovations of such anglers are soon codified into formal schools of thought. Great fishermen are created by the challenge of their favorite rivers, but they also shape the point of view and the methods used on those rivers by the men who follow.

History is filled with examples. Stewart and his soft-hackled wet flies and his upstream school of casting were a response to the swift-water hatches and emerging *Trichoptera* that abound in Scotland. Halford was a product of the mayfly abundance on his chalk streams in Hampshire, and regular fly hatches on smooth currents were the catalyst that produced the dry-fly method. Theodore Gordon was a lonely figure jealously husbanding both his knowledge of dry flies and his frail tubercular lungs through the long Catskill winters.

Gordon was fascinated with Halford and his collation of the chalk-stream hatches and copied a set of dry-fly imitations tied by Halford himself, but Gordon quickly realized that the specific British insects were not found on American waters. Such exact imitation was impossible here when experts in aquatic biology had not yet worked out the classification key of the American genera, let alone classified individual species. He turned to translating the lessons of his British counterparts in American terms, dressing flies suggestive of typical American hatches, while George La Branche adapted the chalk-stream dogma of dry-fly tactics to the swifter streams of this country.

Skues challenged Halford and his disciples for the *ex cathedra* argument that dry flies were the only method worthy of the chalk streams. Skues countered drily that even chalk-stream trout took most of their food in the subsurface or hatching states, and that a delicately fished nymph was no reason for guilt. The argument reached its climax in the famous encounter at the Fly-fishers' in London, when Halford and his curia of faithful disciples cornered Skues.

"Young man," Halford said testily, "you cannot fish the Itchen in the manner you describe!"

"But I've done it," Skues replied softly.

Most knowledgeable anglers are familiar with the writings these men left behind them, and their books are the keystones of fly-fishing literature. But the muse of history is often fickle, and some of our angling giants are half-forgotten across the years.

Our myopic preoccupation with the dry-fly method, through reverence for Gordon and La Branche, has resulted in such an oversight. American anglers have largely forgotten James Leisenring in following the more glamorous heroes of American fly-fishing, but it was Leisenring who quietly adapted the wet-fly tactics of Stewart and Skues to the fly hatches of American waters, just as Gordon and La Branche transplanted British dry-fly methods to the swift rivers of the Catskills.

Leisenring was a skilled toolmaker from Allentown in eastern Pennsylvania, and his home waters were the storied Brodheads and the difficult Little Lehigh, a still chalk-streamlike river nearby. Both streams are a challenge worthy of great anglers, and both are rich in history and tradition. All of the angling giants have fished the Brodheads since its brook-trout beginnings over a century ago. It was the favorite river of La Branche in the years before *The Dry Fly and Fast Water,* and it was home water to Leisenring and his circle of friends—puckishly labeled The Twelve Apostles by the innkeeper who ran the hotel at Analomink.

Leisenring was a tireless prober of secrets along the Brodheads, performing stomach autopsies on trout and collecting its nymph life. His streamside notes were fastidious about color, and he refused to make color judgments about either insects or his artificials except when they were measured *in situ* in the quality of light found on the stream. His observations were gathered in meticulous notebooks of colors and materials.

He fished the river until his death in 1951, ten years after his classic *The Art of Tying the Wet Fly* first appeared. His disciples included famous flytiers like the late Dick Clark and Chip Stauffer, who passed on skills learned from Leisenring to Art Flick on the Schoharie. His portrait was hung by Charlie Rethoret behind the bar of the Hotel Rapids. The hotel and its faithful circle of fly fishermen are gone now, like the Spruce Cabin Inn and the family-operated little hotel at Henryville, which sheltered anglers for six generations before its river holdings passed to a private club.

Pete Hidy is perhaps the best-known of the Leisenring disciples. It was Hidy who helped him in writing his book, and he is again the moving force behind this commemorative edition, adding his own observations on the subtle tactics of matching an emerging hatch.

The little river is still there. Its modern regulars are a skilled breed who have mastered its lessons, and regularly apply the conventional dry-fly tactics of Gordon and La Branche, leavened with terrestrial theories of ants and jassids borrowed from Fox and Marinaro on the Letort. But still there are days on the Brodheads, when the *Trichoptera* and *Epeorus* flies are coming, or the trout are bulging to nymphs and pupae, that the lessons of Leisenring are as fresh as new-minted coins to those who remember.

The new pilgrims will have a fresh opportunity to learn those lessons with the publication of this new edition of *The Art of Tying the Wet Fly,* and those encountering its wisdom for the first time must be cautioned: its lessons are not limited to the Brodheads alone.

Its gentle headwaters still tumble down ledges of rust-colored slate and slide into deep bedrock pools. Tributaries like the Swiftwater and Buck Hill and Cranberry still hold trout deep in thickets of hemlock and rhododendron. There are dancing riffles of bright gravel below Canadensis, and deep ledge pools on the Haase Farm, where April rain trickles down the windows of the farmhouse used by the Brodheads' Flyfishers. There are slow chest-deep runs on the century-old club water, and tumbling pockets and smooth slicks under the spreading oaks and buttonwoods on the Henryville stretch.

Leisenring knew them all during his tenure on the river. The public water he loved below Analomink and Stoke's Mill has been decimated by flood-control work, and much of his fishing took place on pools now leased to private clubs. There are still men on the river who knew Leisenring well, and they smile at the thought of wealthy, modern anglers who use the methods of a simple Pennsylvania German toolsmith without knowing how much they owe that wet-fly wizard of the Brodheads.

ERNEST SCHWIEBERT

Princeton, New Jersey
1970

Selecting Hackles.

FOREWORD TO THE 1941 EDITION

HIGH IN THE RANKS OF PENNSYLVANIA'S trout streams
—possibly at the top—stands the famous Brodheads
Creek. Equally famous as the Brodheads is the Hotel
Rapids on its banks at Analomink, where the genius
of Charley and his wife provides delicious food and
refreshing beverage for anglers and hunters throughout the year. Charley, an accomplished angler himself, is well acquainted with many of the best anglers
in the East, and he can give you offhand the names of
two dozen or so experts with the dry fly. Whenever
the wet fly is mentioned, however, he always remarks,
"Big Jim from Allentown—he is the best we have."
Also, and even when his wife is calling from the
kitchen, he pauses to tell you that for more than
twenty-five years he has seen "Big Jim" take trout—
"those big fellows!"—when even the experts came in
from the stream empty handed.

"Big Jim" is the name of distinction which his
skill as a fly-fisher has brought to James E. Leisenring,
a true Pennsylvania German in every respect. One
afternoon in late June several years ago, I met Jim
for the first time standing at the edge of a great pool
on the Brodheads. He did not see me approach from

downstream because his entire attention was taken by the strategies of a good trout which had just mistaken one of his carefully tied wet flies for a genuine insect. He played his trout perfectly, directing and stemming each rush with a wise touch and understanding, finally netting and wading ashore with his prize, a fat two-pounder.

From this streamside meeting have grown our friendship and my deep respect for this gentle angler who may well be America's most advanced authority on the wet fly. He himself lays no claim to this title. In fact, because of his genuine modesty, he would be the last to accept it. However, for more than a half century he has intelligently pursued the art of flyfishing with remarkable success from coast to coast, casting a dry fly with skill and pleasure whenever the trout would feed at the surface, but recognizing also that the wet fly has still greater possibilities if one would master a technique to search out the trout beneath the surface and force them to feed, so to speak, when the hour or day offers poor sport to the dry-fly-fisherman.

In the following pages the reader will learn, to his surprise, perhaps, that Leisenring's exceptional catches of exceptional trout depend to a large degree upon *small* wet flies which are painstakingly tied with a careful attention to action-giving qualities, size, form and color, and he will learn how they may be fished to appear lifelike and "become deadly," in the words of Leisenring. (Note to theorists: it is not possible to convince this man that trout are color

A rare old photograph of Leisenring taken during the years he fished the streams and lakes of the American West, sometimes supplying trout for the dining rooms of hotels during the tourist season. The well-worn cloth creel over his shoulder would indicate that he was a dependable supplier.

blind or that exact imitation is never necessary; nor will he try to convince you that trout are not color blind or that exact imitation is always necessary. In regard to these moot questions his viewpoint is as flexible as the trout's.)

All flies tied according to Leisenring's directions will prove to be most durable and thus enable the angler to benefit from the increased attractiveness which repeated "gnawing" by trout's teeth gives to all wet flies.

Along with his many admiring friends, it has been my privilege to convince "Big Jim" that his knowledge should be put into book form for American anglers and posterity. He agreed to do it with these words, "All right; I'll write what I know, but you must promise me you'll tell them that I don't expect anyone to agree with a thing I say!"

Having kept my promise to Jim, I must also tell the reader that, in addition to his extraordinary skills as an angler and flytier, this man possesses all of those valuable personal qualities which come to humble men through their fly-fishing days spent with the clean, fresh beauty of game-flavored trout streams. All who know him can truly appreciate those words of Walton, "No life, my honest scholar, no life so happy and so pleasant as the life of a well-governed angler." And, as they consider the completeness of his experience and knowledge in the ways of the sharp-eyed trout, they must say to themselves that if Old Izaak himself were to return and seek out a *Compleat* fly fisherman his search would lead him to Jim Leisenring.

VERNON S. HIDY

Buckingham Valley
Pennsylvania
1941

INTRODUCTION
TO THE 1941 EDITION

SEVERAL YEARS AGO I was busy at my worktable one afternoon when a car bearing Pennsylvania license plates stopped short in a cloud of dust outside the window. A comparatively young man slid out from under the steering wheel, strolled in through the open door and introduced himself as Pete Hidy. He tossed an awfully small nymph on the table in front of me and asked if I could make a couple of duplicates right away so he could get back on the stream where it was doing the trick to the trout.

I paid no attention to the fellow's name and not much more attention to the nymph, as both were complete strangers to me at the time. However, the years have rolled along, as they have a way of doing, and I have learned to have a great deal of respect for Pete and his particular types of nymphs and wet flies as created by himself and Jim Leisenring. I have seen them take trout in Catskill, Adirondack, and Pennsylvania streams where and when a great many other patterns and lures have failed to raise a fish.

The angling fraternity of America has long stood in need of a good book describing the whys and the wherefores of the wet fly, which in recent years has been happily restored to its rightful place in anglers' kits. The wet fly, I am convinced, will take more trout consistently throughout the season than any other type of lure.

It was with keen delight that I learned of *The Art of Tying the Wet Fly* by Pete and Jim, for I know of no other two more enthusiastic anglers more capable at this task.

REUBEN R. CROSS

Lew Beach
New York
1941

Part 1

THE ART OF
TYING THE
WET FLY

I

THE ART OF FLY TYING

ALTHOUGH NOT ESSENTIAL, the fly fisherman can hardly call himself an accomplished angler unless he can dress his own flies with some neatness and exactness to the natural fly. For more than fifty years I have made my own flies and during that time they have been successful in deceiving considerably more than my own share of trout.

As a boy I was forced to make my own flies because they were almost unknown in my locality and I could not afford to send for them in the cities. After fishing with my own flies for some time I secured some "store" flies, but they did not suit my ideas of what a good trout fly should be; so down through the years I have tied my own flies because the commercial products have never possessed the qualities which I sought. Today I still cannot buy flies to equal my own for catching trout, even though most of my fishing is done with a dozen or so old patterns which I carry in different sizes and shades.

Today too many of our flies are tied by wholesale flytiers who don't even fish. This means they are purely mechanical tiers lacking familiarity with the insects which they imitate for fly fishermen who buy their products. I do not mean to say their flies are not sometimes taken, but if the tiers understood and were familiar with the appearance of the *originals* which they copy, certainly they would have a different story to tell.

Another fault of commercial flies is found in the inferior materials and substitutes for scarce materials which manufacturers use in order to meet the prices of competition. A good flytier doesn't care a whit about competition and selects his materials accordingly. As a matter of fact, every flytier worthy of the name would rather not tie a fly than use the cheap substitutes found in many commercial flies. Accordingly, when one desires the finest flies he must pay from four to six dollars a dozen, sometimes more.

Since fine flies are difficult to buy, many fly fishermen tie their own and some have their flies tied to order by professional tiers. A good professional tier usually has orders for many times more than he can produce, for the very good reason that his careful workmanship limits him to three or four dozen flies per day.

The art of tying the wet fly rests upon a knowledge of trout-stream insect life, a knowledge of materials used for imitating the insect life, and an ability to select, prepare, blend, and use the proper materials to create neat, durable, and lifelike imitations of the natural insects.

A true flytier enjoys studying insect life along a stream. I have spent many, many days at it and once put in almost two summers with my friend and companion, Dr. H. W. Lyte, studying one single fly and its nymph until we had it down so it would really catch fish. We called it the Boating Dam fly and it was a "damn" fly until we learned the secret of dressing it.

The art of fly tying is the art of creating an effect, and those of us who tie flies find a great pleasure in making and using our own flies. In the following pages I have given my ideas and methods on the subject of wet flies, but I will advise you to take none of it for granted. Get down to brass tacks by studying the flies on the streams you fish and then duplicate them, creating the general effect with the materials which you believe to be best for it.

If possible, by all means take an early opportunity to observe an experienced flytier at his art. You will learn more by watching him than by reading. And remember that fly tying is an art which requires many months and years to master. As you progress, read and study the other fellow's books and methods. Try them, too; he may have something worthwhile. Magazines, friends, and fishing acquaintances offer new ideas, suggestions, and hints, but the best and most reliable source is you and your personal observation.

At the outset and during the early years of my fly-tying and fly-fishing experience I would have been happy indeed to have had the information contained in this book. I have had much pleasure in gathering and using my knowledge of the wet fly, and it is offered here in the hope that American anglers may find increased pleasure in tying and fishing the wet fly.

TOOLS FOR FLY TYING

At Left: MAGNIFYING GLASS for examining barbs and points of hooks, materials, natural insects, etc.

FLY-TYING VISE into which the hook is clamped tightly while fly is tied.

At Right, from top to bottom:

HEAVY HACKLE PLIERS which, when clamped to the end of thread or tying silk, give necessary tension to the tying silk when its use is interrupted by other operations, selection and preparation of wing materials, etc., before the fly is completed.

SHORT HACKLE PLIERS used for winding hackles.

QUILL STRIPPER used for removing the tiny fibers from edge of peacock quills.

FLY-TYING KNIFE, fine pointed and razor sharp, for close, neat cutting.

QUILL for applying lacquer or varnish.

SCISSORS, fine and straight pointed, with holes large enough for a man's fingers.

TWEEZERS, wide pointed, for preparing bird hackles.

TWEEZERS, fine pointed, for picking up hooks, dubbing, quills, hackles, etc.

HATPIN, short, for picking out dubbing, cleaning lacquer from eyes of hooks, and over which tying silk is suspended out of the way during other operations.

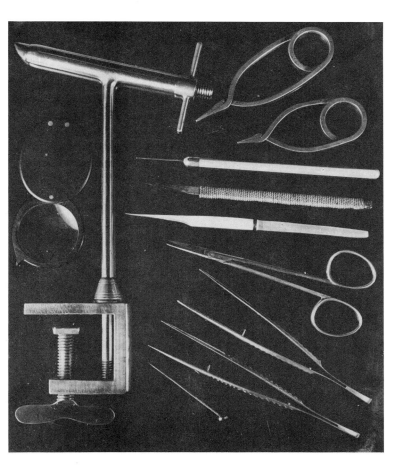

2

TYING SILK

A MOST IMPORTANT AND NECESSARY item for a flytier is a fine, strong tying thread. It must be fine in order to allow neat work and it must be strong in order to make a durable fly. Every flytier who wishes to make neat, durable flies will do well to choose his thread carefully.

The ideal thread which meets all the requirements, to my way of thinking is Pearsall's Gossamer "Fly-Dressing" Silk. It is sold on convenient little fifty-yard spools and is available in several desirable colors. I would recommend purchasing the following colors and quantities: Primrose (color #3)—2 spools; Claret (color #13)—1 spool; Gray (color #9a)—1 spool; Hot Orange (color #19)—2 spools; Brown (color #17) —1 spool; Plum (color #8)—1 spool; and Green (color #18)—1 spool. The numbers are from Pearsall's chart or sample card.

A strong tying silk is doubly important because a very important fundamental of tying a durable fly is this: *always keep your thread taut.* At no time during the tying of a fly should you allow the least bit of slack in the thread. When this happens your fly is likely to be a loose affair and parts of it may slip out from under the thread. A taut thread is especially important at the vital operations such as tying in the hackle, tail, rib, body, wings, and the whip finish. Form the habit of keeping the thread taut at all times. Thread well waxed with the type of wax described here will not slip and unloosen very quickly even if the tension is relaxed momentarily, but the best policy is to form the habit of keeping your thread taut at all times regardless of the advantage good wax gives you.

Great care must be taken in tying in the parts of your fly and then fastening off your work securely with the invisible knot or whip finish at the eye of the hook in the final operation. It is a big mistake to assume that a very fine tying silk enables you to take more than the necessary number of turns in tying a fly. Whenever a tier puts more turns of silk in his flies than are absolutely necessary, he is either in the production game or just careless.

With a well-waxed tying silk under a good tension during the construction of a fly, half hitches are unnecessary. They do not improve a fly, and a fly finished off with a dozen half hitches needs varnish or lacquer. When the varnish wears off the fly will come untied. The best and ideal method of finishing off a fly is the invisible knot or whip finish. A well-waxed thread with a three- or four-turn whip finish will hold without varnish or lacquer, and flies which I tie for my personal use are seldom lacquered. However, my advice is to lacquer the heads of all flies for the additional protection and durability.

The color of tying silk should be chosen to harmonize with the body materials you intend to use in imitating a particular insect, keeping in mind the *undercolor* which you wish to show out through and reflect from the dubbing or body of your completed fly.

3

WAX

WAXES FOR FLY TYING are like hooks—there are all
kinds. The wax which I have found to be entirely
satisfactory is made according to an old recipe of J.
Harrington Keene's, as follows:

Melt one-half pound of the best white turpentine
resin, add one ounce of pure white beeswax which
should be pared off or chopped up into small pieces.
Simmer for fifteen minutes, allowing it to melt and
mix thoroughly with the resin. Now add one-half
ounce of fresh lard and stir slowly while the mixture
simmers just below the boiling point for another fifteen minutes. (Note: when stirring this simmering
wax remember that it is extremely inflammable and
therefore dangerous. The safest and best stirring im-
plement is a stick about eighteen inches long and
somewhat smaller in diameter than a lead pencil.)
Pour this liquid wax into a basin of water. *Do not
touch it until it has had a chance to cool* because your
fingers will be badly burned. After it has cooled
enough to permit handling, pull at it and work with
it, as taffy pullers do with taffy, until it has a light
color and even texture. You will find it necessary to

41

immerse it in warm water in order to make it pliable enough to work.

Remember that a batch of this wax will last for years, so make it right while you are making it. Roll it into pieces about the size of hickory nuts, wrap them in wax paper and store in a cool place.

When using this wax do not use a piece bigger than a BB shot because you will likely break the fly-tying thread using it. Before waxing your thread, moisten your thumb and forefinger and work the piece of wax between them to soften it somewhat.

Drawing your thread against the wax between your fingers will give you a thread stiff enough to prevent twisting and just sticky enough to grip well against the hook, accepting the tension given and somehow sealing itself onto the hook, a most valuable aid to a fly's durability.

This wax on your thread will often leave a tiny speck of wax on the head of the fly after the whip finish is completed. This tight wrapping of the thread over itself and the pulling through necessitated by the whip finish causes this. I always remove this speck of wax with my dubbing needle with the satisfaction of knowing that, unlike the half hitches used by some, that whip finish is there to stay. And they do stay. This is a perfect wax for tying durable wet flies.

4

THE HOOK

A VITAL PART OF EVERY GOOD FLY is the hook upon which it is tied. The finest flies would be worthless if tied on cheap or inferior hooks. In recent years there has been an avalanche of cheap hooks on the market in general, and therefore the wise fisherman will look twice before buying his hooks.

My own personal demands of a hook are these: a reasonably fine wire, an exceptionally good temper, a good hollow point, fairly long to stand repeated sharpening with a hone, and a small, nicely tapered barb which will allow the hook to slide in easily instead of having to be set into the tissue of a fish's mouth or jaw with a severe yank or jerk to put it in over the barb.

The overlarge barb is one of the serious causes of losing fish. Often you may hook a nice trout, play him a while, and then suddenly find the fly coming toward you and the fish going in the other direction. Eight times out of ten, I assure you, the barb of your hook was not deep enough into the fish's flesh. You simply had the point of the hook stuck into him up to the barb. As long as there was a fair amount of tension on your line it held him, but as soon as he got slack line he was able to eject the fly. Any hook that is set over the barb into that gristle or tough flesh is not going to be dislodged very quickly by any trout, even if he does manage to get slack line. Most hooks sold today have a barb so wickedly big that, even if you do manage to set it into a fish's jaw without breaking your gut leader, the barb makes such an enormous gash or hole when it enters that it becomes as easily dislodged as a hook which has not penetrated over the barb.

A hook's shape is largely a matter of opinion. Personally, I prefer a round bend secured for me by Messeena's of London, England.* These hooks leave nothing to be desired. They may be seen in the photographs of my flies in the chapter on Fly Patterns and Dressings. My next choice is a hook which I used to get from Allcock's in a sproat style: #1810 First Grade Hollow Point. I have not been able to get these lately but they are excellent hooks, far superior to Allcock's #1810 Best Grade Hollow Point. Of course, there was sixty cents difference in the price per hundred but I am not interested in cheapness—it is quality I am after and I will gladly pay for it.

All hooks for my own use are straight, without side bends or snecking. If I want them bent to the side I bend them to suit myself with a pair of jewel-

---

* Now incorporated with E. Veniard, Ltd., 138 Northwood Road, Thornton Heath, England CR48YG.

ers' pincers which I carry in my vest pocket. Also, I prefer my hooks to have turned-down eyes.

I do not use snelled flies any more because a fly tied on gut is of very little value during the second season. Besides, the habit snells have of becoming twisted together just when you want a fly quick is enough to drive any fisherman mad. If your flies are tied on eyed hooks it gives the advantage of being able to carry about four times more flies in even less space than is required for snelled flies. Also, a fly on an eyed hook can be changed in half the time it takes to change a snelled fly. I am convinced that trout of today are so well educated that a leader knotted with looped snells cannot deceive them unless manipulated with exceptional skill. For the eyed fly you can select the exact size of gut tippet needed or advisable at any time for whatever situation faces you. Years ago, when more worthwhile trout could be caught on almost any size of leader or fly, these considerations were not important. Today, the difference between 3X and 4X gut, or the difference between a size 12 and a size 14 fly often may, and does, mean the difference between catching fish and not catching them.

Most flytiers and anglers are of the opinion that all wet flies should be tied on comparatively heavy hooks, but I have found it advisable to tie many of my favorite patterns on light wire hooks in order to achieve a better similarity of movements and sinking qualities characteristic of many insects. Also, it permits me to fish my wet flies on the surface, a procedure which is often very effective. Of course, if I desire a fly to sink quickly, as many of them should, I simply use a hook with heavier wire, but the quality and specifications of the hook must remain the same. Messeena's get these hooks for me in two different weights according to my specifications. They will accept and fill your order for hooks of any size, shape, quality, or weight according to your needs or desires.

Experience has taught me the extreme importance of keeping hook points needle sharp. For many years I have used a small, hard, and smooth Arkansas whetstone for touching up the points of my hooks. This is a stone such as jewelers and engravers use for sharpening their engraving tools, and it does not give a wire edge to your hooks or wear them away as do the cheap carborundum hook hones on the market.

5

HACKLE

IN SELECTING HACKLES for the wet fly it is necessary to keep in mind that the trout prefers his food alive. Live insects kick their legs and struggle. They also possess an iridescence, a liveliness of color which vanishes when they die. Therefore, the careful flytier will select his hackle according to its ability to *act* and *look* alive.

To make a fly appear alive and kicking it is necessary to select a stiff, medium, or soft hackle according to the water to be fished—that is, hackles of stiff fibers for swift, fast water; hackles of medium quality for slower water; and hackles of soft quality for slow water. Thus the fly-fisherman takes advantage of the variations in hackles and fits them to variations in water to get lifelike action.

To give artificial flies the iridescence of the living, natural insect, it is necessary to select and use hackles that reflect light. The word "glassiness" best describes this quality, and it can be identified by holding the hackle to the light. A little examination and study of the natural insects along a trout stream will explain the importance of this quality.

Poultry hackles may be obtained from the farmer's barnyard, the poultry stores, or material supply houses. The poultryman will usually give you permission to pull hackles from his stock, and he will save the heads and necks for you if you will pay him something for his trouble. I find that poultry hackles are at their best when plucked in February and March.

A rare and valuable hackle is the blue dun. My search for hackles has brought me one, sometimes two good blue dun cock birds every five or six years. Some flytiers raise their own blue dun fowl or pay a farmer to raise them, just for their feathers. A good honey dun bird is almost as rare, so make the most of their feathers when they come to your attention.

Always look carefully at the underside of hackles before taking them. Often an apparently good brown hackle will be "chalky" or much paler on the underside. This is undesirable. Select hackles which have an equal or nearly equal tone of color on both sides.

Dressing or changing winged flies into hackle patterns rests upon two considerations—color and place or position, first, of the wings and, second, of the legs. You must select a hackle that combines as far as possible the color of the wings and legs, and if you keep these colors in their positions it will matter little to the fish whether the fly has wings or not. Take for example a fly that has dun or lead-colored wings and yellow legs. By choosing a hackle with a blue or dun list and yellow tips you imitate both the wings and the legs, because the blue or dun list represents the wings and the yellow tips represent the legs. Another example is the Dotterel Dun, a fly which represents a light, yellow-legged dun. The dotterel hackle is a brownish dun feather with yellow tips to the point of the fibers, and the dun color represents the wings while the yellow tips represent the legs. The Iron Blue Dun is imitated with a dun-colored feather which has reddish tips.

Here are the names and descriptions of hackles as I use them in this book and in my fly tying:

FURNACE—Has a very dark, black, or blue dun list next to the stem and on the tips of the fibers. In between the dark list and tips is a good color, usually a red, yellow, white, or silver. The hackles which show these three distinct markings are known as furnace hackles and the name, such as Red Furnace or Cochybondu, Yellow Furnace, etc., is determined by the color between the dark list and tips.

BADGER—Also has a dark list and colored fibers but here the color of the fibers extends from the list clear to the tips of the fibers. Thus the Badger differs from the Furnace in that the dark list does not reappear on the tips of the fibers. The name of a badger hackle, such as Yellow Badger, Silver Badger, etc., is determinded by the color which extends from the list to the tips.

GRIZZLY or CREE—Barred or mottled hackles from the barred Plymouth Rocks.

BLUE DUN—A smoky gray color from the palest pearl gray to the darkest blue gray.

RUSTY BLUE DUN—Same as Blue Dun except that it

has a rusty or reddish appearance when held up to the light.

BRASSY BLUE DUN—Blue Dun with a yellowish tinge.

HONEY DUN—Has a gray or blue dun list with honey-colored fiber ends. When the list is dark the hackle is called a Dark Honey Dun and when the list is light the hackle is called a Light Honey Dun.

Here are a few definitions of value to the flytier:

BUFF—A dull, light yellow color.

TAWNY—Name of composite color consisting of brown with a predominance of yellow or orange. Formerly applied to other shades of brown—a light tawny or yellowish red.

DINGY—Of a disagreeably dark and dull color or appearance; formerly applied to naturally blackish or dusky brown color but now applying to a dirty color or aspect due to smoke, grime, dust, weathering, or deficiency of daylight and freshness of hue.

BLOA-BLAE—Literally the color of a dark, threatening sky; dark gray or bluish gray.

DUSKY—Somewhat black or dark in color.

DUN—A name for various dusky-colored flies used in angling, and for artificial flies imitating these. "Dun is the mouse." Dusky, dingy.

The following hackles are useful to the flytier:

RED FURNACE or COCHYBONDU

YELLOW FURNACE

PALE or WHITE FURNACE

BADGERS—Red, yellow, brown or chestnut, and pale.

GINGERS—Lightest to dark.

GAME HEN—Plain red, cinnamon, buff, badgers and furnaces.

BARRED PLYMOUTH ROCK cock hackles.

BLACK

BLUE DUN—Both cock and hen from darkest to palest.

HONEY DUN

OLIVES—Yellow olive, brown olive, greenish brown olive. (Must be dyed with fast dyes.)

BIRD HACKLES

Valuable hackles necessary for certain patterns of flies are secured from the wings and bodies of such birds as the following:

COOT—These hackles are found in the marginal coverts on the outside of the wings, and on the under-coverts inside of the wings.

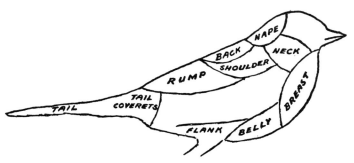

Location of Bird Hackles

GROUSE—The European grouse furnishes some very good rich brown speckled feathers from the wings and back.

JACKDAW—The cock bird gives us the hackle for the deadly Iron Blue Dun Nymph. These hackles are a dark, smoky blue and very useful. Purchase a whole neck skin.

LAND RAIL—These hackles are all most useful. For some of the Sedges they are absolutely necessary. You will find them both inside and outside of the wing, but purchase the entire bird if possible.

PARTRIDGE—The English or Hungarian partridge provides the flytier with some valuable gray and brown speckled feathers from the wings and breast of the bird. Valuable for March Browns and Sedges.

PLOVER—The golden plover supplies a very good hackle for some flies. The feathers are speckled between a dark ash color and a yellow.

SNIPE—These hackles are found in the marginal coverts on the outside of the wings, and in the undercoverts inside of the wings. Best hackles come from under the wings of the jack snipe in the undercoverts.

STARLING—Select your hackles from the skin of the male bird. I think the starling has the finest hackles you can use for the gnats and small spiders. For the Black Gnat you will find exceptionally good ones on the shoulder of the bird. These are blackish purple, fairly large, and they possess iridescent fibers which give your fly a most lifelike appearance. There are not many blackish purple hackles on a bird—about twenty-five to each shoulder. These hackles come clear

OUTSIDE OF WING   *Jack Cameron*

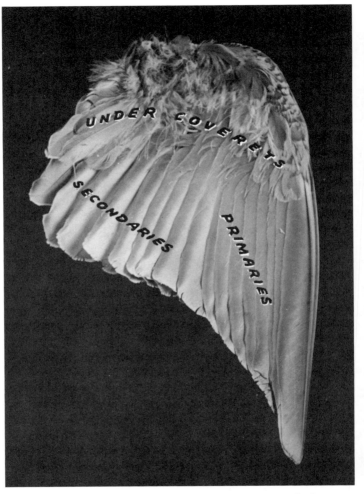

INSIDE OF WING   *Jack Cameron*

down around the neck and remind one of the ruff on a grouse when a starling struts around. Immediately behind these feathers you will find some larger hackles which have a bluish green iridescent sheen and also make a killing gnat or spider. The nape of the starling's neck also has some very good hackles of a rich, deep purplish black.

One of the best substitutes for the dotterel hackle is found among the undercoverts of the starling wing. These feathers are dun colored with buff or yellow tips, and can be distinguished from the genuine dotterel only by a difference in stiffness. All of my flies made to fish for the Dotterel Dun are made with this hackle because it is next to impossible to secure the true dotterel. I used to import the dotterel skin for my own use but lately it has been protected and kept from the trade.

WOODCOCK—The English woodcock provides some very good hackles useful for making spider flies, dark March Browns, and Sedges. These hackles are found on the back and wings.

6

BODY MATERIALS

SINCE THE BODIES OF MOST TROUT-STREAM insects are somewhat translucent the flytier must choose materials to imitate them with qualities which produce or reproduce those little sparkles of light which transmitted light gives to the bodies of natural insects. The bodies of natural flies allow a certain amount of light to pass through them, so we may understand the effectiveness of furs and herls as body materials, since they also permit light to pass through them. Bodies of such opaque materials as quill or raffia grass must appear quite dark and unnatural to a fish below unless the fish sees the fly by light reflected from the stream bed. My experience has taught me that bodies of artificial flies are most deadly when, in addition to color, they imitate the texture, translucence, and flash of the natural fly as nearly as possible.

Furs which I have found most useful are: seal, mole, red fox, Australian opossum, marten, squirrel, bear, muskrat, field mouse, and English hare's mask.

The fine woolly down under the bristles of a pig is exceptionally good for making a rough-bodied fly. It is very transparent and gives off bright, snappy color effects. Black, white, and red can be secured in natural colors. The reds are especially good for spinners and the white is easily dyed any shade. Dye some pig's wool a claret color for Claret Duns and Spinners. This material spins fairly well and makes a wonderfully translucent body which retains its luster and color when wet.

Worsted of desirable colors and shades may be secured from the remnants of discarded Turkish carpets. This material is hard and glassy, just the thing for the famous Cowdung fly as well as all the rough-bodied caterpillar tribe. Every flytier should secure some worsted, even if he must steal it from his wife's carpets. The colors are fast and, unlike silk, change but little when wet.

When ordering hare's fur, ask for the hare's mask, which means the skin from the whole head. A flytier has use for the whole mask because the ears, the poll (between the ears), the face (between and below the eyes), and the cheeks are of different color and quality. Remove each type of fur from the mask and keep each separate in strong envelopes labeled and protected by a little moth preventive, because this particular material seems to hold an unusual attraction for moths as well as trout. The American hare and the American rabbit are worthless for tying the famous Hare's Ear fly.

Another good body material is herl. Peacock herl, especially the pure bronze-colored, is a fine material and is used in my dressing of the Red Hackle and Gray Hackle, probably the most killing general-purpose flies I have used through the years. Use great care in selecting this bronze herl because it is quite rare. You will probably be forced to buy a package of magenta dye and dye some of the common greenish herl in order to achieve the true bronze effect. Here are some pointers in testing herl for the genuine bronze: hold it to the light. If there is any greenish tinge, try another feather. If you find a feather with a true bronze appearance, hold it to the light, turn it in your hand and slant it so that light is reflected from various angles on and through its fibers. If you find a feather that passes this test without showing the least bit of greenish tinge you will have the genuine bronze herl. Bronzy green and bright green herl are also desirable body materials. The fibers of the peacock secondary wing feathers make a fine pale-blue-dun body.

Herls from the fibers of large black feathers such as turkey, raven and crow secondaries make killing bodies for tiny Black Gnats. (Use two or three strands of herl, tie them in at the bend of the hook with a tying silk of the *undercolor* desired, and wind them up the hook together with the tying silk which is twisted in with the herl and thus enabled to show through evenly, at the same time adding to the durability of the body.)

Raffia grass is an excellent body material. It should be dampened before using in order to make it pliable enough to work neatly.

Quill of various kinds is available to the flytier. Quill stripped from the stems of wing feathers is used by many for certain flies. To my mind stem-quill is of little value because it possesses no translucence and a fly tied with it must depend entirely upon reflected light for its color effects.

Condor quill is fairly good and I use quite a bit of unstripped condor quill because it gives translucency by means of the tiny fibers on the side of the quill; also, it gives the effect of segments. Those tiny fibers act very lifelike by quivering as the current acts upon them.

A two-stripe quill, to make such flies as the Olive Quill, Ginger Quill, Quill Gordon and Blue Quill, is secured from the peacock eye, or the tip of the peacock tail feather which is known as the eye. To judge a peacock eye for quality quill, take the eye between thumb and forefinger of the left hand pretty well toward the end of the fibers. Holding it tight in the left hand, grasp the stem of the eye with the thumb and forefinger of the right hand, just below the heart-shaped marking on the eye, and twist. You can then see the whiteness of the quill in the eye.

Before your peacock quill is ready to be used as a quill body you must strip it, that is, remove the tiny fibers which are on the black edge. The best way, to my knowledge, of stripping quill came to me from my fishing partner, Mr. Albert Kraft, a true angler and a fine flytier. One day while driving to the Poconos to tempt some of those educated brown trout with our flies, after several miles of the usual conversation two fly fishermen will carry on, I said, "Pete, don't you know of anything new to talk about?"

"Why yes," he answered, "I know of a new way to strip peacock quill." He then told me to get a fine sewing needle, a fairly thin one, and stick it into the end of a small, thin piece of wood for a handle. This is best done by gripping the needle with a pair of pliers in order to force it securely into the wood. Insert the needle eye-first into the wood about three-eighths of an inch, leaving about seven-eights of an inch protruding. This is your quill stripper. Now take a piece of smooth cardboard such as the politicians hand around at election time and lay it on the edge of your worktable. Take up the small end of the quill, grip it in your hackle pliers in order to turn it from side to side easily, and lay it on the smooth card. Take up the quill stripper now and press it firmly down on the quill near the hackle pliers, being careful to hold the needle squarely across the quill, not at an angle. Now simply pull the quill through under the needle, keeping an even pressure with the needle against the quill. After that, turn the quill over and repeat the operation if necessary, and it is ready for use, thoroughly cleaned and undamaged. I do not know where Pete picked up this most useful trick, but it is a very good one and I am certainly glad to know about it.

A valuable body material which I use in dressing the Tup's Nymph and the Snipe and Yellow is yellow buttonhole twist. This material takes on a greenish tint when wet, and I also use it for ribbing the Old Blue Dun because it blends with the blue muskrat fur to produce a most lifelike olive color. This buttonhole twist* is sold on little ten-yard spools by dry goods stores and department stores.

Better than the buttonhole twist available today (1970), however, is Pearsall's Marabou floss silk, which is available from Veniard in England in both primrose and light yellow. For small flies, use just one of the two strands that are twisted together on the spool.

An important task of the wet-fly tier is blending furs, hair or wool and spinning them on a desirable color of tying silk in order to produce the desired effects. To do this well requires a knowledge of materials as well as a knowledge of the natural insect. In the chapter on Fly Patterns and Dressings I have indicated the color of tying silk to be used in tying the fly as well as for spinning the body.

While speaking of materials it is well to remember that furs and feathers should be placed in envelopes and cedar boxes and kept where sunlight or bright light may shine upon them. You should then have very little trouble with moths, because moths do nearly all of their dirty work in the dark. Remember that an evildoer loveth darkness (this also applies to very big trout). Also, take your furs and feathers out of the containers once in a while and shuffle them,

---

* You may use the primrose tying silk described in Chapter 2 as a substitute. By doubling it and twisting it you will have the desired thickness for ribbing the Old Blue Dun.

changing their position. Use paradichlorbenzene crystals; or a few drops of cedar leaf oil (not oil of cedar) will do the trick.

Fly-making materials can be secured from houses which make a specialty of handling them, but it is almost impossible to get good, genuine materials from the lower class dealers. The beginner is advised, therefore, to buy his materials from dealers of an established character and reputation. The following is a list of fly-tying-material supply houses where I purchase many of my materials. These houses are reliable and you can be assured of getting the genuine article.

E. Veniard, 138 Northwood Road, Thornton Heath, Surrey, England. CR4 8YG

E. Crawshaw and Company, 286 Goswell Road, London, England.

E. B. and H. A. Darbee, Livingston Manor, New York.

Buszek's, 805 W. Tulare Avenue, Visalia, California.

E. Hille, Williamsport, Pennsylvania.

Fireside Angler, Melville, New York.

7

SPINNING A BODY

THE PURPOSE OF THIS CHAPTER is to explain the best method of spinning a body which will stand up under the gnawing of trout's teeth. A body which has been scraped down and worn well—practically worn out—is better than a new one for catching fish, so it is well to construct them for long wear.

You may begin to spin a body by taking a small amount of dubbing in the palm of your hand, laying it a little thicker at one end to give it the proper taper. Wet the second finger of your right hand, place it on top of the dubbing and roll it until you have a little, solid and tapered roll. Fasten the small end at the bend of the hook with your tying silk, which must be well waxed, and then, laying the dubbing against the tying silk, press them together so that the dubbing will adhere to the waxed silk. Twist them a little and wind the two-in-one result up the hook shank to the desired length of body.

However, a body spun in the following manner is practically indestructible, enables the flytier to spin the hard, wiry materials such as seal's fur without difficulty, and gives the fly a good undercolor through the medium of your tying silk.

Take a piece of fly-tying silk nine or ten inches long, of the desired color which you wish to show up in the body as undercolor, and wax it well. Lay it lengthwise on your left leg right in the middle on top, from your kneecap back, as in the photograph. Let one-third of the thread hang down over your knee in front out of the way. Now take the dubbing to be spun and spread it along the waxed silk thread, starting about two inches from the end of the thread nearest to your hip. Spread it sparsely at first, evenly and gradually increasing the amount in order to have an even-tapered body for your fly. About one-and-one-eighth inches is long enough for a size 12 or 13 hook, but after spinning a few and using them you will be able to judge the desired lengths for various hook sizes pretty accurately yourself.

Now we have our silk lying in a straight line and our dubbing spread out properly to make a neat, tapered body. Now place the thumb of your left hand on the bare silk about one inch from the end nearest your hip. Place the second finger of your left hand on the bare silk beyond the dubbing toward the knee.

With the thumb and first finger of your right hand grasp the silk hanging over the knee; bring the silk up and pass it or pull it under the second finger of your left hand, being careful not to release the pressure on the silk held down by thumb and finger

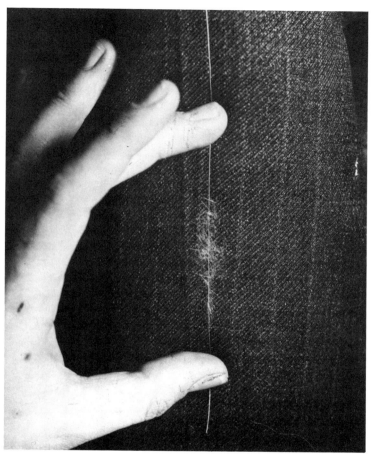

First step in spinning a body: waxed tying silk stretched along leg at knee with proper amount of dubbing placed on top of thread or tying silk.

Jack Cameron

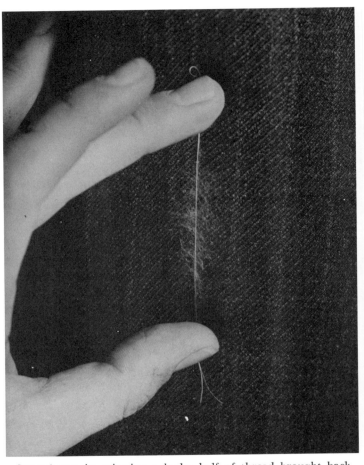

Second step in spinning a body: half of thread brought back and down against dubbing in line with bottom half, thus trapping dubbing between the two halves of one thread.

Jack Cameron

of your left hand. Keep the thread and dubbing straight and tight.

Now that you have your silk pulled under the second finger, place the first finger of your left hand on top of both threads and within one-half inch of the dubbing. You now have the thumb, first finger, and second finger of your left hand on the silk. Remove the second finger, keeping a good pressure on the ends of the thread beneath the dubbing with your first finger and thumb.

Holding the end of the loose thread between the thumb and forefinger of your right hand, bring this thread down directly on top of the bottom thread so that the dubbing is in between these two well-waxed threads. Before touching it to the dubbing, however, stretch it tight and then make sure the top thread is absolutely in line with the bottom thread.

Now use the second finger of your right hand to press down the top thread against the dubbing directly in front of your left thumb. Hold it there, remove the left thumb, slide the finger toward the two loose ends of silk and replace your left thumb.

At this point remove your right hand from the scene of operations and observe the two silk threads with your dubbing between them, the first finger of your left hand holding the threads down at the end nearest your knee and your left thumb pressing down just behind the dubbing.

Take the doubled end of silk at your knee between the thumb and first finger of your right hand and

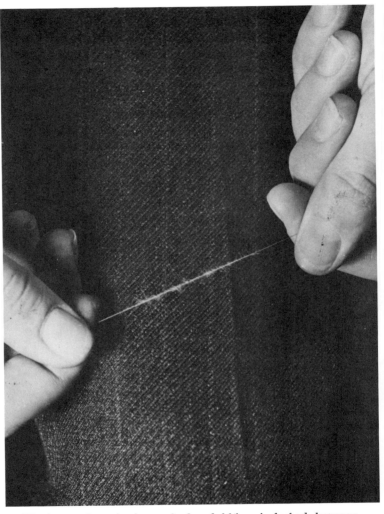

Final step in spinning a body: dubbing is locked between threads by twisting ends in opposite directions.

Jack Cameron

pull at it in order to get the loop out straight. Let it go and lay it flat down on your leg. Then take your thumb and put it on top of the doubled silk at right angles to it. Press down lightly and, starting with the heel of the ball of your thumb, pull your thumb

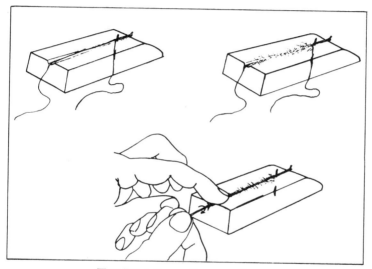

THE DICK CLARK SPINNING BLOCK

A longtime Leisenring pupil, companion and friend invented this device for using Jim's method of spinning dubbing between two threads without the use of sophisticated fingering or an untidy trouser leg. The waxed thread is looped over the headless brads and secured in knife-cuts in the close-grained hardwood block leaving both hands free to arrange the dubbing. Then the right-hand thread is laid over the dubbing along the shallow groove, and all are twisted to make a fly body. Block shape and dimensions are not critical but everything, particularly the cut-off brads, must be sandpapered glass-smooth.
Drawing by Eugene Arnold, Jr.
Courtesy of Anglers' Club of New York

across the silk, thus rolling the silk that is under it. Give it two or three such rolls, holding it down each time, until it is twisted tight.

After you give it the last roll, catch it up and give it another roll or twist between the thumb and forefinger. Stretch it toward the knee and lift the left forefinger straight up off the silk, keeping the thumb down tightly on the opposite end. As you lift the left forefinger the silk and dubbing will twist into a rope, so to speak.

Being careful to keep the thread twisted and taut, catch up the threads under your left thumb and twist them in the opposite direction.

Now, holding the completed spun body in front of you, you see that it consists of two heavily waxed threads which have trapped the dubbing between them by being twisted together.

At this point I have a number of light cardboard cards, 2¾″ x 4″, notched for holding the bodies. I put twelve little cuts down each side of the card, spacing them evenly and cutting each about ¾₆″ deep. I make the cuts on the edges with my pocketknife or scissors. By putting the thread ends of the spun body into the notches, stretching the body across the card, one has a neat, clean and convenient method of storing bodies until needed. I usually keep on hand a few dozen spun bodies such as hare's ear, mole, red fox, field mouse, seal's fur, opossum, muskrat, etc., which are spun in my spare moments and stored in a box until needed. When I wish to tie a few flies the bodies are ready. I usually replace them soon after they are used.

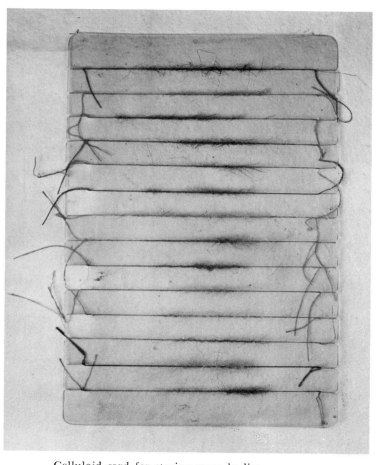

Celluloid card for storing spun bodies

Jack Cameron

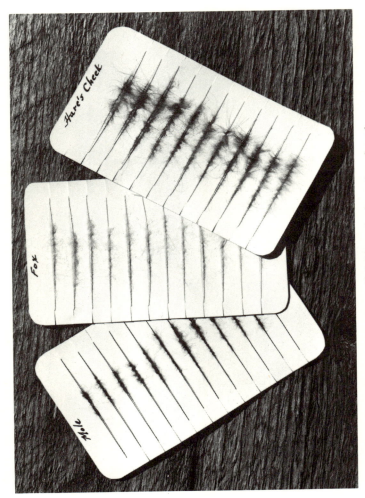

Spun bodies on celluloid cards for tying flymphs.

This manner of spinning a body gives in my opinion the best and most durable body it is possible to use in the construction of a fly. Such a spun body wears for an unbelievable length of time and the dubbing does not pull out because it has become a part of your tying silk.

If you grasp the knack of spinning bodies in this manner, I believe you will agree with me that it is the easiest and simplest way possible, unless one is on a production basis and is not concerned with the durability of his flies. Remember to twist the body again and in the right direction as you wrap it about the hook shank. Although leaving them on the card tends to set the waxed threads, they will unwind slightly when removed.

To learn this method of spinning a body it is best to practice with a piece of silk thread heavier than the tying silk, size A for instance, and, say, some muskrat fur. Practice spinning several bodies until the method is thoroughly understood, being careful to taper them nicely, and adapt the length to the size of hook on which it is to go.

After mastering the method, you will occasionally spin a body that is not well done. Throw it away. Good enough is not good enough for a conscientious flytier. Make your bodies perfect and have the satisfaction of knowing they are perfect. The body is the most important part of a wet fly.

8

WING MATERIALS

MY EXPERIENCE IN TYING and fishing artificial flies has shown and proven to my own satisfaction, as well as to many of the finest fly fishermen I know, that the wing is the least important part of a fly. True enough, some patterns are more effective if tied with a wing, but I could always, and still can, catch more fish on a wingless imitation.

When choosing material for winging a fly it is important to remember that the wings of most natural flies are transparent—you can actually read print through them. Artificial wings should have a similar quality to be a successful rendering of the natural. Most flytiers wing their flies with the web of the mallard wing feathers, a material of such thickness and stiffness that I do not use it, even though it is easy to tie and inexpensive.

The ideal wing material is that which has the transparency, thinness, pliableness, and markings of the natural insect's wings. Most of what I consider the best winging materials will be found in the primaries and secondaries of the wings which I have recommended for bird hackles in the chapter Hackle. In addition to those, hen and cock blackbird wing feathers are needed in tying the Greenwell's Glory. Partridge tail feathers have a rich, reddish brown color useful for wings of Sedge flies. Game hen primaries and secondaries are useful in tying the March Brown and Alder. Coot wings possess the right brownish tinge for many of the stone flies. The sides and flanks of the wood duck or mandarin provide a light or medium brown speckled feather.

It is important for the flytier to understand that some wings are glassy and transparent, while others are not. The wings of newly hatched duns are dull and of a smoky color whereas the mature dun, or spinner, has wings that are glassy and transparent. Therefore it is advisable for the flytier to imitate this effect to the best of his ability, since the trout is often selective enough to feed on but one type of fly even though there are others on the water at the same time.

When imitating a newly hatched dun's wings, I tie in the wing material with the dull, upper side of the web to the outside. When imitating the wings of a spinner, I tie in the wing material with the shiny, underside of the web to the outside. Hackle tips provide a very good imitation of the spinner's wings.

The wings of sedges or caddis flies are thin and transparent, and the wings of stone flies and Yellow Sallies are quite transparent. The alder resembles the sedges but has a good color and a bright, glossy sheen to its wings, well represented by the shiny underside of speckled game hen secondaries.

9

MY METHOD OF TYING A FLY

TO EXPLAIN MY METHOD of tying a fly this chapter is devoted to a detailed, step-by-step description of the operations and considerations I believe necessary to construct a neat and durable fly. The pattern to be tied for illustration is the Blue Dun Hackle, one of my favorite flies, and before beginning it is necessary to have at hand the following materials:

HOOK   12, 13, or 14.

SILK   Primrose yellow.

HACKLE   Light blue dun hen hackle of good quality.

TAIL   Two or three blue dun fibers.

RIB   Very narrow flat gold tinsel.

BODY   Mole's fur spun on primrose yellow silk.

Plate I illustrates the process of establishing a firm, tight beginning after the hook is placed in the vise. Having waxed the thread, figure 1 shows the beginning turns. When within about 1/16″ from the eye of the hook, bring the thread back across the last turn as in figure 2 and wind three tight-fitting turns back away from the eye. Unwind the short end of the thread up to where it is covered as in figure 3, cut it off with the scissors, and you are ready for the opera-

PLATE I

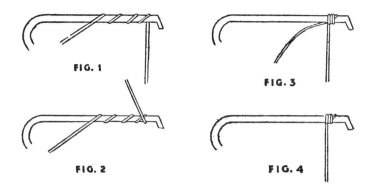

FIG. 1

FIG. 3

FIG. 2

FIG. 4

tion of tying in the hackle, having completed a neat, firm and tight beginning as in figure 4.

Before tying in the hackle it is well to understand how a poultry hackle is prepared and what happens to the stem when the useless fibers are stripped off. Every beginner experiences difficulty in winding hackles neatly, but if the construction and preparation of a hackle is understood, then neat hackle winding becomes a comparatively easy matter.

In Plate II, figure 1 shows a poultry hackle intact, just as it is plucked from the neck of any common domestic rooster. Figure 2 shows the same hackle, with the useless fibres stripped off, ready to be tied in against the hook shank.

As you will notice, in figure 2 two more fibers have been removed from one side of the feather than from the other. The reason for this is explained in

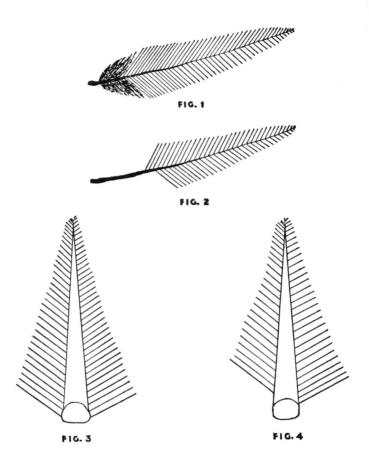

FIG. 1

FIG. 2

FIG. 3

FIG. 4

PLATE II

figures 3 and 4 where an enlarged cross section of the stems shows their construction and appearance before and after the useless fibers have been removed. Figure 3 shows the rounded edge of a hackle stem before the fibers are stripped off. Figure 4 shows the flat edges of a hackle stem after the useless fibers have been stripped off. The edge with the two extra fibers removed from it is the edge which goes against the hook shank as the hackle is wound on; and, in order to have that edge come against the hook shank as you begin the first turn, it is necessary to tie in your hackle with the underside or duller side of the hackle away from the hook, and the upper or shiny side of the hackle next to the hook. Thus it is obvious that in the stripping off of the extra fibers they will be removed from the side near to you if the hackle is held by the tip in your right hand with the dull side of the hackle toward the floor and the shiny side facing up. After removing the extra fibers, turn the hackle over with the shiny side against the hook and it is ready to tie in.

The photograph illustrates the preparation of a bird hackle. At the top is a whole bird hackle. Next is shown the hackle with the fluff and unwanted fibers stripped away and with two or three extra fibers removed on one side to facilitate winding as explained above. Grasp the tip end of the hackle in the fine forceps or tweezers and stroke all of the fibers so that they slant back toward the butt end of the hackle stem. Hold the lower stem of the hackle in your left hand, moisten the thumb and forefinger of your right hand with saliva, and then, grasping the few fibers that were covered by the forceps, roll them between

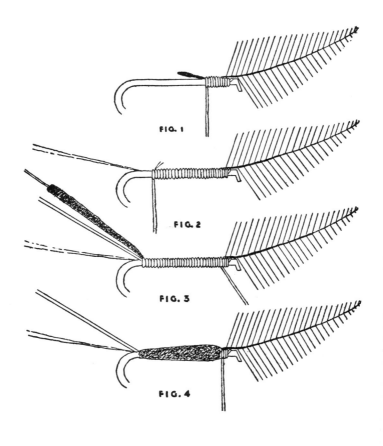

FIG. 1

FIG. 2

FIG. 3

FIG. 4

PLATE III

the moistened finger and thumb. Release the butt of
the hackle from your left hand and you can give the
tip a nice roll between your fingers. The final step is
accomplished by taking the hackle stem in your left
hand again and stroking the fibers in opposite directions with the forceps straddling the stem until it
appears ready for use as at the bottom of the photograph. Keep the tip matted together with saliva and
rolled so that the hackle pliers may hold while winding the hackle, remembering that bird hackles are
tender until wound on. I always tie them in at the
quill end instead of the tip and find that they stand
up under extreme abuse from the trout.

Plate III shows the hackle tied in with six or
seven turns of tying silk as in figure 1. Clip off the
butt of the hackle stem with your scissors and continue winding your tying silk in close, tight turns
down to the point shown in figure 2 where the tail
is tied in. Next tie in your tinsel ribbing material
and, finally, the spun body as shown in figure 3, after-
ward bringing the tying silk in close, tight turns up
to the hackle. Now stick your pin in the edge of the
table, attach the heavy hackle pliers to the end of your
thread and throw the thread over the pin so that it
hangs to the right at an angle of about 45 degrees, out
of your way, with the hackle pliers keeping tension
on it while you wind on the body.

Now take a little rest, look at your work, and see
if everything is as it should be according to figure 3.

When you are ready again, start winding the
body of spun mole's fur, twisting it about every one-

Web cut from two feathers taken from opposite wings.

Jack Cameron

and-a-half turns in order to keep everything tight. When you have brought up the body to a point just behind the hackle, tie it off with three turns of tying silk and cut off the unused part of the body, if any, with your scissors. After you have spun a few bodies you will get used to judging lengths so accurately that it will be unnecessary to cut off surplus body material.

After tying off the body, your fly should appear as in figure 4.

Preparation of a bird hackle.

Jack Cameron

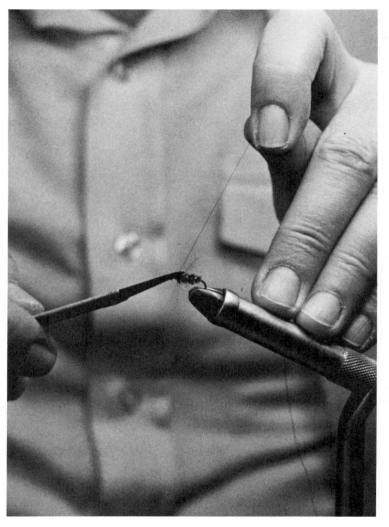

Fly-tying knife used for cutting off the surplus tying silk after the invisible knot or whip finish has been completed.

Lance Hidy

The next operation is ribbing the body. I usually take one or two turns of the tinsel around the bare hook under the tail and then proceed to wind it in spirals up the body as in Plate IV, figure 1, to the

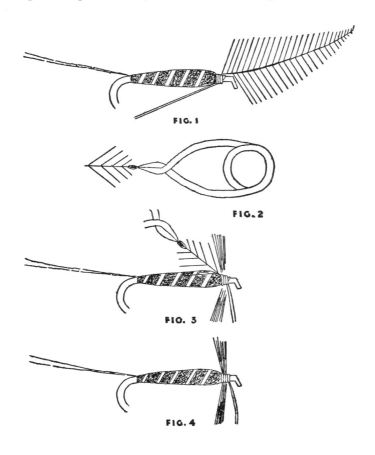

FIG. 1

FIG. 2

FIG. 3

FIG. 4

PLATE IV

point where the body was tied off. Now take three or four turns of tying silk over the tinsel, winding in the direction of the bend of the hook or tail of the fly and keeping tension on the tinsel with your left hand. Now take the tinsel in your right hand, bend it back and forth, giving it somewhat of a circular twisting motion and it will break off readily. (With wire ribbing the twisting motion is not necessary.) Tinsel or wire cut off with scissors often pulls out from under your tying silk so take the little extra time needed to twist it off, noticing the rough edge which remains and holds it securely.

Before grasping the hackle in your hackle pliers, arrange your thread over the pin to your left so it will be out of your way while you wind in the hackle. Figure 2 illustrates the best method of gripping the hackle tip in the hackle pliers, either poultry or bird hackle. Having gripped the hackle, raise it up as shown in the photograph so that the first turn can be started on the flat side of the stem where the two extra fibers were removed when you prepared the hackle. When this is done you will find that the hackle readily adjusts itself in the proper position, starting itself around edgewise as it should. Proceeding slowly, take two, two-and-a-half, or, at the most, three turns of the hackle about the hook, winding in the direction of bend or tail end of the fly. Now take the tying silk and bring it over the final turn of the hackle and up through the fibers with two or three turns to make your hackle secure while being held at a tension with your hackle pliers in your left hand, as in figure 3.

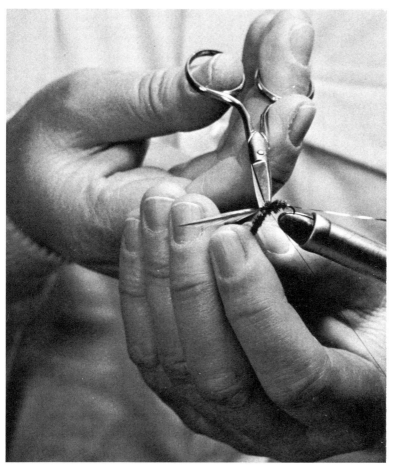

Scissors used for cutting off surplus peacock herl after body is completed.

Lance Hidy

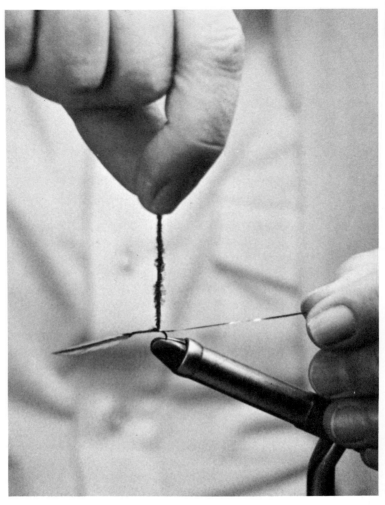

Ribbing tinsel is held out of the way in the left hand while the right hand brings the peacock herl (three strands knotted at end between fingers) over and down to be twisted with and wound up the body with the tying silk.

Lance Hidy

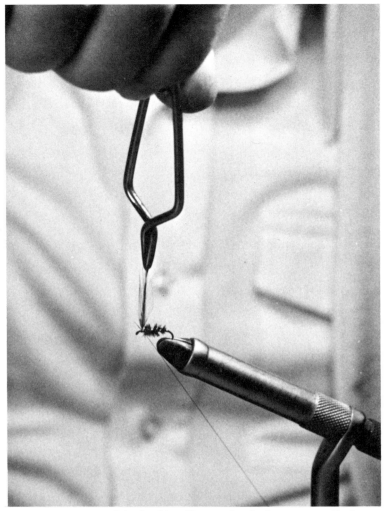

Hackles gripped in hackle pliers and raised to perpendicular before beginning the first turn in winding hackle.

Lance Hidy

Next, gently pull the hackle tip left in the hackle pliers up and away so that you may get at the stem to cut it away with the fly knife. The knife does a much neater job than the scissors because with it there is no danger of cutting the hackle fibers. Keep a slight tension on the hackle tip held in the pliers and cut it off fairly close to the point where the first turn of your thread is wound over the hackle. After the tying silk is wound up through the fibers and the hackle tip is cut off, your fly should appear as in figure 4.

The final operation in tying a fly is the whip finish, or invisible knot, illustrated in Plate V. Figure 1 shows a loop thrown into the tying silk so that the thread may be wound over itself three or four turns as in figure 2. After taking the turns, place your pin through the loop as in figure 3, pull the loop straight up and keep a tension on it with the pin as shown in figure 3. Taking the thread in your left hand, pull it carefully until the top of the loop is drawn down against the hook, withdraw the pin and pull tight as in figure 4. Apply lacquer or varnish and your Blue Dun Hackle is complete.

When finishing off the head of a fly you can also wind your thread in close turns clear to the eye and back again tight against the hackle, jamming the first few fibers back slightly, before tying the whip finish.

When tying the whip finish be sure the loop is thrown as illustrated in figure 1. If the loop is not right you will not get a whip finish. The beginner will do well to practice the whip finish on a bare hook until he grasps the idea of it. It is the best fastening that can be made, and is also used for winding on fly rods since it is absolutely secure and very neat.

PLATE **V**

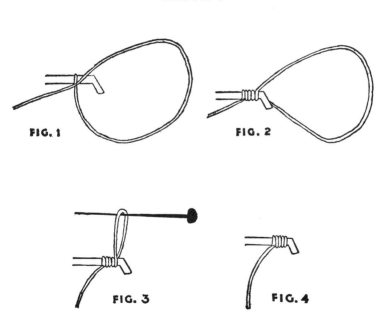

FIG. 1

FIG. 2

FIG. 3

FIG. 4

The palmer fly is simply a fly with an extra hackle which is tied in at the tail and wound spirally up the body as in Plate VI. Tie in the tip of the hackle, wind it in long spirals up the body, cut off the butt with your scissors, and tie down the butt with two turns of tying silk. If flat tinsel or round wire is used in ribbing a palmer fly, I find it best to

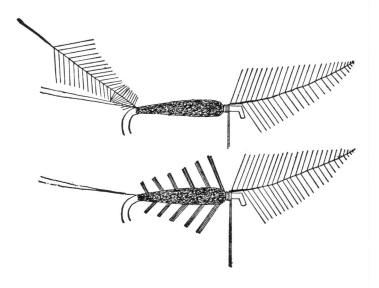

PLATE VI

rib right in front of the hackle all the way up. After breaking off the tinsel I apply a small amount of lacquer or varnish to the tying silk after cutting the hackle butt away to make it a little more secure. Do not put too much on as it will penetrate into the body. Let it dry for two or three minutes and wind in the other hackle, finishing off with the whip finish as usual.

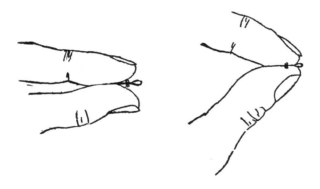

PLATE VII

When tying wings on a fly it is necessary to allow sufficient space for the wings by starting the thread back farther in the beginning operation so that the wings may have a base of three or four turns of tying silk as illustrated in Plate VIII. This foundation must lie back far enough from the eye to allow room

for finishing off after the wings are tied in, a fact
often overlooked by beginners.

Since the wings must match, it is necessary to cut
one piece of web from a right wing feather (as illustrated in the photograph) and the other piece of web
from a left wing feather. Cut each piece of web from
$\frac{1}{8}''$ to $\frac{3}{16}''$ in width and lay them together, shiny
sides in or dull sides in, according to whether the fly
is to represent a dun or a spinner. Hold them between
the thumb and forefinger of your right hand and
place them down in between the hackle so they reach
back to the bend of the hook or a little beyond, rest-
ing down against the bed of tying silk. Now grasp the
wings with the thumb and forefinger of your left hand
and hold them in place firmly as illustrated in figure
1 of Plate VIII where the dotted lines represent the
thumb and forefinger which must hold the wing in
position while it is being tied in.

By the illustrations in Plate VII you may understand what takes place now as the thread is brought
up between the thumb and wing and passed down on
the other side between the forefinger and wing. Practice will show you how the gap between the ends of
thumb and forefinger may be opened and closed without loosening or changing the position of the wing
against the hook. It is necessary to open this gap to
bring the thread up between the thumb and wing on
the first turn and you will find that the end of your
thumb can be moved out enough to allow the thread
to pass up through without moving the forefinger
away from the wing on the opposite side. Similarly,

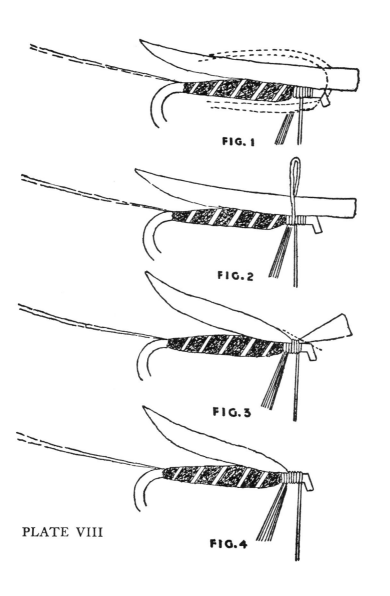

FIG. 1

FIG. 2

FIG. 3

PLATE VIII

FIG. 4

after the thread has been brought up between the thumb and wings, you will find that the end of your forefinger can be moved out enough to allow the thread to pass down without moving the thumb away from the thread against the wing on the other side. This is the trick to tying a perfect wing.

The first loop should be about ¾" high as illustrated in figure 2 of Plate VIII. With a reasonable pressure against the material with the thumb and forefinger of your left hand, pull gently and straight down on the thread in your right hand so that the loop is drawn down against the wing material on its bed of tying silk. You must pull this loop down squarely or you will separate the fibers of your wings and they will set unevenly on the hook. Again pass the thread up between the thumb and wing and down the other side between the wing and forefinger, getting this second turn just ahead of the first. Pull the loop down tight again, repeat the operation for the third time and when the thread is taut remove your thumb and forefinger, since the three firm, even turns of silk will hold your wings in position. Keep your tying silk taut and cut the wing stumps off along the dotted line with your scissors as in figure 3. Now wind the tying silk in close, tight turns over the stumps to the eye, as in figure 4, and back again to your first turn over the wings. Make the whip finish from this point, apply a drop of lacquer and your fly is completed.

No beginner can tie a decent wing at first. However, careful practice and a study of what takes place between your fingers as the thread is pulled down will soon teach the knack of it. Don't give up after the first failures and don't be satisfied until your wings are straight and perfectly tied. Practice winging flies by sitting down with nothing but thread, wing materials and a bare hook in the vise. When you have tried one set of wings, cut them off, thread and all, with an old knife blade, and try again. Once you have mastered the trick you will have it forever.

10

NYMPHS

ANGLING WITH THE ARTIFICIAL NYMPH is one of the most interesting and effective methods of catching fish known to man, as well as the least understood in the minds of fly fishermen. On the stream, natural insects come up out of the water, hatching from nymphs, and fly about in the air near the water where we may study their behavior and characteristics; but nymph life exists under the water in another world, so to speak, of gravel, stones, weed beds, and natural debris where the eye cannot see. Therefore the angler is forced to adopt certain methods of learning the secrets of nymph life if he wishes to take fish with his artificial nymphs.

My method of studying nymphs is a simple one calling for a few of the white, semiopaque dishes sold in five-and-ten-cent stores (known as opal glass), a magnifying glass, pencil, and notebook. After catching a trout, open his stomach and put the contents in the small, flat-bottomed dish, add a little water and stir with your finger to separate the good specimens of nymphs and insects from the digested matter. Remove the good specimens, rinse out the dish, replace your specimens and add about ⅟₁₆″ of clean water. Now you have an ideal setup for using your magnifying glass, pencil, and notebook in learning the trout's diet and making a record of it for future reference. I have several of the small dishes hidden along the streams I fish, having found it more convenient to hide them than to carry a single one with me always.

Nymphs may be caught in a cheesecloth net by holding it downstream from a weed bed while your fishing partner stirs through the weeds and turns up some stones. This will dislodge some of the nymphs and the water will carry them down into your net. By reaching under the water and picking up stones, especially flat ones, you can find many nymphs, because many types of nymphs live on stones until they are mature and ready to hatch into the winged insect.

If you will be very quiet and stand still, you may watch trout digging nymphs out of the gravel and weed beds. They will even move small stones to get at them; and if you tie fairly good representations of the specimens you should catch trout. My experience has led me to believe that the trout is not so particular when he goes nymphing. He will often take any nymph he can dislodge, case and all.

Trout often feed on nymphs at or near the surface as they hatch into the fully matured insect and leave the water to fly. At such times the fly fisherman is up against a different proposition, because the hatching nymph is usually of a certain size, shape, and color, and the trout will often stick to that one type in their feeding. If it is an Olive Dun you will usually be required to use an Olive Dun nymph of the same size or a little smaller. If they are caddis or sedge flies you will be required to use a nymph to represent these. Then, if the fish change off to a diet of the mature fly which flies over and rides the surface of the water, it will probably be advisable to use a dry fly or fish a wet fly on the surface.

I am of the opinion that a good many patterns of flies have the faculty of representing or suggesting both the nymph and fly stages of certain insects—if they are tied right. Such a fly is the Gold Ribbed Hare's Ear. The dark-blue-hackled Iron Blue Dun also has this faculty if it is tied with a hackle possessing a dark-blue center, or list, and reddish or yellowish tips to the fibers. The Hare's Ear is especially good, with or without the gold rib, when the sedges are on the water and hatching out. I use an English woodcock wing feather for winging this fly because it has a bar lacking in our American woodcock. By taking one of these sepia-colored secondary feathers with the buff bar, I dress my Hare's Ear with a buff tip to their wings and find it very effective.

Now, in nymph fishing your hook must be exceedingly sharp, so sharp that the fish hooks himself or almost hooks himself when he takes your nymphs. The pressure of the water and the drag caused after he takes the nymph does this if the hook is as sharp as it should be. The very point of your hook coming in contact with the flesh or inside of the fish's mouth will engage, and he can't immediately get rid of the hook until you feel him. This will enable you to set your hook in over the barb and all will be secure. More fish are lost because of dull, cheap hooks than all other causes combined, so the wise fisherman will look well to his hooks.

Since nymphs are fished deep, the hooks for them should be of heavy wire so they will sink deep. I have no use for a weighted nymph because they do not swim naturally.

Plate IX and Plate X illustrate the step-by-step procedure I follow in tying the Tup's Nymph, a nymph that catches fish throughout the season.

Before beginning to tie this nymph it will be necessary to have at hand the following materials:

HOOK	13, 14.
SILK	Primrose yellow.
HACKLE	Very small light-blue hen hackle or medium-dark honey dun hen hackle.
BODY	Halved: rear half of primrose yellow buttonhole twist; thorax or shoulder of yellow and claret seal's fur mixed dubbing spun on primrose yellow silk.
TAIL	Two honey dun hackle points.

In Plate IX, figure 1 shows a very short-fibered hen hackle tied in, and the tying silk brought down the hook shank to a point where the primrose yellow buttonhole twist body material is tied in. Figure 2 shows the body material tied in and the tying silk

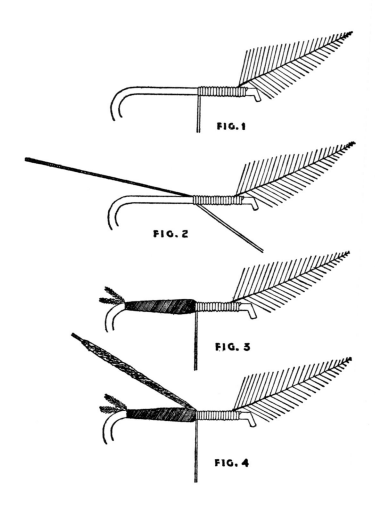

FIG. 1

FIG. 2

FIG. 3

FIG. 4

PLATE IX

extended to the right out of the way where it will remain while the body and tails are tied in. Do not
bring the waxed tying silk down the hook shank any
farther than shown, because we want the body to
be as transparent as possible. (You cannot see through
the body after the nymph is finished—don't expect
that. But when it becomes wet and water-soaked it
becomes somewhat transparent if there is no waxed
tying silk under it to make it opaque.) So, then, the
body will be composed of the buttonhole twist, using
one or two of the three strands in the thread.

Take the buttonhole twist and wind in close
turns down the hook shank, taking care to keep the
two hackle point tails on top of the shank and winding over them at each close turn until you reach a
point opposite the barb of the hook. Then wind the
material back in close turns up to the tying silk, fasten
with the tying silk, clip off the surplus material and
the work should appear as in figure 3.

Next, tie in the thorax close against the body as
in figure 4.

Plate X, figure 1, shows the tying silk brought
up to the hackle and extended over a pin to the right
out of the way while the thorax is wound on. Wind
the thorax in close turns right up to the hackle and
tie it off with two or three turns of the tying silk.
Bring the tying silk over to your left out of the way
and your work should appear as in figure 2.

Take the hackle in the hackle pliers and wrap two
or, at the most, three turns of hackle right over the
fastening-off silk and up against the dubbed body.

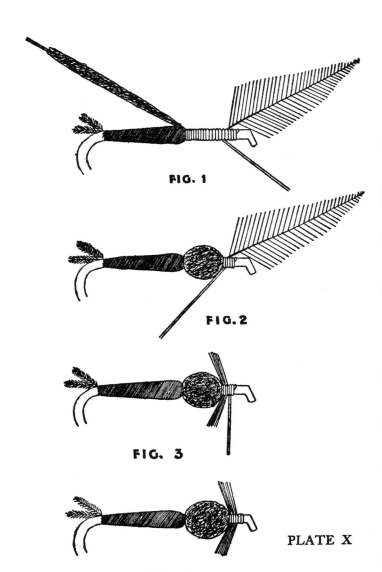

FIG. 1

FIG. 2

FIG. 3

PLATE X

FIG. 4

Take your thumb and forefinger and—with the flesh, not the nails—jam or push against the hackle so that it is forced back against and almost into the dubbing. Now bring your tying silk over the hackle end, wind over and on top of it two or three turns, bringing the tying silk up through the hackle toward the eye, and the work should appear as in figure 3.

Take the hackle fibers between your thumb and forefinger and hold them back out of the way while you wind your tying silk in tight turns halfway to the eye and then return right back to the hackle, jamming one or two turns right up against the hackle. Be careful not to run the silk over itself; make each turn fit neatly against the other.

Now finish off the nymph with the invisible knot or whip finish and your Tup's Nymph will be completed as in figure 4.

This is the best all-around nymph I have found.

In addition to the Tup's Nymph and the Iron Blue Nymph, I have found the following patterns effective in taking trout.

MARCH BROWN NYMPH

HOOK	13.
SILK	Orange.
HACKLE	A short-fibered, light brown feather from the Hungarian partridge.
TAIL	Three fibers from a cock pheasant tail feather tied very short.
RIB	Gold or silver wire.
BODY	Three reddish fibers from a center feather

of a cock pheasant's tail. (As with peacock's herl, tie in, twist with thread, and wind up body, twisting together as you go.)

THORAX   Hare's ear fur dubbed fairly heavily.

Half Stone Nymph

HOOK   13, 14.
SILK   Primrose yellow.
HACKLE   Very short blue dun hen's hackle, 2 turns or 3 turns at the most.
TAIL   None.
RIB   Very fine gold or silver wire.
BODY   Primrose yellow buttonhole twist.
THORAX   Mole's fur dubbed fairly heavily.

Dark Olive Nymph

HOOK   14, 15.
SILK   Primrose yellow.
HACKLE   One or not more than two turns of the tiniest blue dun hen's hackle.
TAIL   Two or three very short, soft blue dun cock fibers.
RIB   Fine gold wire.
BODY   Dark green-olive seal's fur mixed with a little dark-brown bear's fur (found next to skin) spun lightly at the tail and quite heavily at the shoulder or thorax.

Pale Watery Nymph

HOOK   15, 16.
SILK   Primrose yellow.

HACKLE   One or not more than two turns of a dark-ish-blue cockerel hackle only long enough to suggest wing cases.

TAIL   None.

RIB   Fine gold wire halfway up the body.

BODY   Cream-colored fur (Chinese mole or Australian opossum) dubbed very thinly at the tail and heavily at the shoulder or thorax.

PALE WATERY NYMPH—effective when light-colored duns are on the water.

HOOK   15, 16.

SILK   White, waxed with colorless wax.

HACKLE   One turn of a very short honey dun cock hackle.

TAIL   Three strands of very short, soft-blue-dun cock fibers.

RIB   None.

BODY   Undyed seal fur or pale buff Australian opossum fur dubbed lightly at the tail and thicker at the thorax.

JULY DUN NYMPH

HOOK   15, 16.

SILK   Orange waxed with colorless wax.

HACKLE   One turn of a very short, soft-rusty-dun cock hackle.

TAIL   Three fibers of a ginger hen's hackle tied very short.

RIB   Fine gold wire halfway up the body.

BODY   Darkish-brown-olive seal fur.

THORAX   Medium-dun mole fur.

II

FLY PATTERNS AND DRESSINGS

THERE ARE ENTIRELY TOO MANY PATTERNS of flies for
me to attempt even a brief description here. Other
books have described and pictured them by the hun-
dreds, but it is my belief that relatively few of
these patterns ever see action on the stream. If we
were to choose two of each pattern and carry them in
two or three different sizes, we would be so burdened
and encumbered that we could not get very far with
our fishing. Then too, if one were to hunt out a particular pattern from this mess, he would not have
time left for his fishing.

Assuming that a fly fisherman usually carries a
few different patterns of flies, it is important that he
choose them in various sizes and let his choice of patterns be governed by the time, district, and water he
intends to fish. Every experienced fly fisherman knows
that trout streams and even separate sections of one
stream often show definite variations of insect life
which he must well consider, to be sure of his sport.

After one possesses a sound selection of patterns
in various sizes, all tied with care and attention to

those qualities discussed in previous pages, the angler's further pleasure and success depend largely upon the presentation of his flies to the trout, a subject which is discussed in the chapter "Fishing a Wet Fly."

While fishing a stream, especially an unfamiliar one, it is always advisable to consult the local anglers, who often tie their own flies and are the source of some killing patterns or variations of standard patterns effective in their neck of the woods.

As every fly fisherman has his favorite patterns, here are mine with their detailed dressings:

BROWN OR RED HACKLE
HOOK   12, 13, 14.
SILK   Crimson or claret.
HACKLE   Red furnace.
RIB   Narrow gold tinsel.
BODY   Bronze-colored peacock herl.

GRAY HACKLE
HOOK   12, 13, 14.
SILK   Primrose yellow.
HACKLE   Yellow or white creamy furnace.
RIB   Narrow gold tinsel.
BODY   Bronze-colored peacock herl.

OLD BLUE DUN
HOOK   12, 13, 14.
SILK   Primrose yellow.
HACKLE   Blue-dun hen hackle of good quality.

TAIL — Two or three glassy fibers from a rusty-blue-dun cock's hackle.

RIB — One strand of yellow buttonhole twist.

BODY — Muskrat underfur spun on primrose-yellow silk, a little of the silk showing through dubbing at the tail.

WINGS — Starling optional.

BLUE DUN HACKLE

HOOK — 12, 13, 14.

SILK — Primrose yellow.

HACKLE — Light-blue-dun hen hackle of good quality.

TAIL — Two or three blue-dun fibers optional.

RIB — Very narrow flat gold tinsel.

BODY — Mole fur spun on primrose-yellow silk, a little of the silk exposed at the tail.

COACHMAN

HOOK — 12, 13.

SILK — Orange.

HACKLE — Bright red cockerel hackle.

BODY — Bronze-colored peacock herl.

WINGS — Land rail, primary or secondary.

BLACK GNAT

HOOK — 14, 15.

SILK — Crimson or claret.

HACKLE — Purplish black feather from the shoulder of a cock starling.

BODY — Black silk or two or three fibers from a crow's secondary wing feather.

WINGS   Dark starling optional.

HARE'S EAR
HOOK   13, 14.
SILK   Primrose yellow.
HACKLE   None: a few fibers of dubbing picked out
          for legs.
TAIL   Two or three fibers of the fine mottled
          feather of a wood duck or mandarin duck.
RIB   Very narrow flat gold tinsel.
BODY   Fur from the lobe or base of a hare's ear
          spun on primrose-yellow silk.
WINGS   English woodcock secondaries with buff
          tips.

IRON BLUE WINGLESS
HOOK   14, 15.
SILK   Crimson or claret.
HACKLE   Honey dun hen hackle with red points, or
          a very dark honey dun.
TAIL   Two short dark honey dun cock fibers.
RIB   Fine gold wire optional.
BODY   Dark mole fur spun on crimson silk; very
          thin at tail to expose silk.

LIGHT SNIPE AND YELLOW
HOOK   13, 14.
SILK   Primrose yellow.
HACKLE   Snipe from the undercovert feathers or
          lesser covert feathers.
RIB   Fine gold wire.

BODY   Primrose-yellow buttonhole twist.

Pale Watery Dun Wingless

HOOK   12, 13, 14.
SILK   Primrose yellow.
HACKLE   Pale honey dun.
TAIL   Two or three pale honey dun cock fibers.
BODY   Natural raffia grass, lacquer optional.

Tup's Nymph

HOOK   13, 14.
SILK   Primrose yellow.
HACKLE   Very small light-blue hen hackle or me-
            dium-dark honey dun hen hackle.
BODY   Halved: rear half of primrose-yellow but-
            tonhole twist; thorax or shoulder of yellow
            and claret seal fur mixed dubbing spun
            on primrose-yellow silk. (See Tup's Nymph
            under chapter on Nymphs.)

Iron Blue Nymph

HOOK   14, 15.
SILK   Crimson or claret.
HACKLE   Two turns of a very short cock jackdaw
            throat hackle.
TAIL   Two or three soft white fibers tied very
            short.
BODY   Dark mole fur spun on crimson or claret
            tying silk with two or three turns of the
            silk exposed at tail.

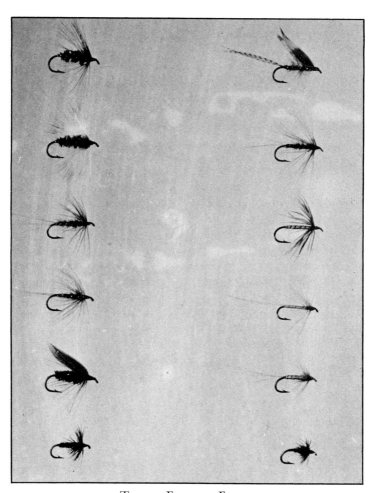

TWELVE FAVORITE FLIES

BROWN OR RED HACKLE	HARE'S EAR
GREY HACKLE	IRON BLUE WINGLESS
OLD BLUE DUN	LIGHT SNIPE AND YELLOW
BLUE DUN HACKLE	PALE EVENING DUN
COACHMAN	TUP'S NYMPH
BLACK GNAT	IRON BLUE DUN

Jack Cameron

Those are the twelve flies with their dressings and sizes which I rely upon. I call them my "favorite twelve" because they have proven to be dependable fish-getters. Of course, I carry and use, occasionally, many others; but the above twelve are the ones and the only ones I can rely upon to get fish most of the time.

Here is a very good little fly I have found at times very deadly. The dressing was given to me by one of my fishing companions, an expert flytier, Dr. H. W. Lyte, of Allentown, Pennsylvania, with whom I have spent many most pleasant days studying the natural fly and its imitation on many streams.

DOCTOR LYTE PALMER

HOOK	13, 14.
SILK	Orange.
HACKLE	Pure honey dun of rich color and medium stiffness—two turns.
RIB	Fine peacock herl of the sword feather—one of the long, thin fibers.
RIB #2	Very narrow gold tinsel wound right alongside of the peacock herl rib and in front of it.
RIBBING HACKLE	Pure honey dun hackle slightly smaller than the front hackle.
BODY	Dingy-orange worsted wool.

I have found W. C. Stewart's spiders to be a deadly combination on every stream I have ever fished. If a fly fisherman presents them carefully, he

Other Excellent Patterns

DOCTOR LYTE PALMER	MARCH BROWN
STEWART'S BLACK SPIDER	GREAT RED SPINNER
STEWART'S RED SPIDER	ALDER
COWDUNG	WATERY DUN

STONE

can soon acquire the reputation of a fish hog! The dressings for the black, the red, and the dun are given below. After tying in the hackle by the stem, Stewart put the tying silk against the stem on the inside of the hackle, twirled them together slightly, and then wound them about the hook shank together.

BLACK SPIDER

HOOK	14, 15.
SILK	Tawny brown.
HACKLE	Purplish black starling feather.
BODY	Waxed tying silk.

RED SPIDER

HOOK	14, 15.
SILK	Primrose yellow.
HACKLE	Land rail.
BODY	Waxed tying silk.

DUN SPIDER

HOOK	14, 15.
SILK	Primrose yellow.
HACKLE	Dotterel or imitation dotterel.

The six flies described below are often valuable to the wet-fly fisherman.

The Cowdung is not a water-bred fly but it is blown into the water and taken eagerly by the trout in streams flowing through meadows where cattle are grazing. If the weather is open they appear from

March throughout the season and they may be seen in various sizes clustered on every cow dropping. The wings are almost transparent and should be imitated with the land rail feather that has the pinkish tinge of the natural fly. The body should be dressed rather full and rough.

COWDUNG

HOOK	12, 13.
SILK	Orange.
HACKLE	Ginger hackle similar to the color of the body.
BODY	Yellow crewel wool, seal fur or mohair mixed with a little brown fur to soften the glare and give the whole a dirty orange tinge.
WINGS	Land rail slightly longer than the body and sloping back close to the body, glossy side out.

The March Brown appears from the beginning of May and lasts until the end of June, according to the locality. Each fly lives for three or four days as hatched and then changes into the Great Red Spinner which is found around the water for several days longer.

MARCH BROWN

HOOK	10,12.
SILK	Orange.
HACKLE	Brown partridge back hackle.
TAIL	Partridge tail fibers.

RIB   Unwaxed tying silk.
BODY   Medium hare's ear for the male, and dark
           hare's poll for the female.
WINGS   Hen pheasant secondaries or partridge tail
           feathers.

GREAT RED SPINNER
HOOK   10, 12 long shank.
SILK   Claret.
HACKLE   Bright amber-red hackle.
TAIL   Three whisks of bright amber-red hackle.
RIB   Fine gold wire.
BODY   Reddish brown pig's wool spun on claret
           silk.
WINGS   Land rail or rusty-dun hackle points

ALDER
HOOK   13, 14.
SILK   Crimson.
HACKLE   Rusty black or blue-black cock.
WINGS   Speckled game hen secondaries tied well
           down along the body, glossy side out.

WATERY DUN
HOOK   14, 15.
SILK   Primrose yellow.
HACKLE   Ginger hen hackle.
TAILS   Ginger cock fibers.
BODY   Hare's poll or buff Australian opossum
           spun on primrose silk.
WINGS   Pale starling.

The stone fly is a good morning and evening fly and is especially good on dark, gloomy days.

STONE

HOOK	10, 12 long shank.
SILK	Primrose yellow.
HACKLE	Brownish red cock hackle in front of wings.
TAILS	Two fibers of a mottled partridge tail spread and tied very short.
RIB	Yellow silk.
BODY	Yellowish brown mohair mixed with light hare's ear fur.
WINGS	Two dark rusty-dun cock hackle points tied flat on the back and extending a little past the body, or two dark-gray mallard feathers tied flat and long.

The stone fly cannot be well represented unless tied with wings. The body should be tied long and fairly thick, as broad at the tail as in the middle. The color of the body is a very light brown broken at intervals with light-yellow joints or ribs between the segments, showing much more yellow on the belly than on the back. This fly has two small feelers on his head and two short, heavy tail fibers. When full grown the stone fly has two pairs of wings which lie flat on his back and are slightly darker than the color of his back.

12

FISHING A WET FLY

I HAVE OFTEN BEEN ASKED THE QUESTION: "Why do you usually make good catches and mostly big trout when you are fishing? We fish with you, ahead of you, or behind you, and it makes no difference. For goodness' sake, what is your secret? Do you live a charmed life, or what is it? Have a heart, Jim, and let us in on your secret."

Well, I assure you that I have a heart and my life is not charmed by any means. Nor have I any dark secrets. I have nothing which I would withhold from my fellow anglers; I just am not built that way.

Here are my ideas on how a fly should be fished. Judge for yourself whether there is a secret or charmed life about it. I know of nothing more enjoyable than going on a fishing trip, unless it would be sitting down to a good meal, and I would have to think twice before deciding which of the two I enjoy more. Fly fishing and the men who do it can best be explained as Dr. Thayer of Baltimore once explained them to me when I was a patient under his care.

One morning he came to my bed and looked

down at me. "Jim, do you know that you are crazy?"

"Oh, my God!" I thought.

"Don't look at me so. It's true," he replied.

"How do you, an intelligent human being, mean that?" I said finally.

"Well, you are," he said. "You fish, don't you?"

"Yes, I do."

"Well, that's why you are crazy. We are all crazy and can't get away from it. If you walk down the street people look at you and say: 'There goes one of those fishermen. He is crazy to fish.' If you walk along the street again and someone else sees you, they will say: 'Look at that fellow. He doesn't fish or want to know anything about fishing. He is crazy or he would go fishing.' So you see, Jim, you are crazy no matter how you take it."

I believe the learned doctor was right. We are crazy. Although I was a dangerously sick man I enjoyed this incident very much. Dr. Thayer was as fine a man and sportsman as I have ever known to caress a fishing rod.

Now, if I want to catch a trout, first I must know where there are some to catch, or neither you nor myself can catch any. If I want to catch a big trout I must first locate a big one or be content with smaller ones. It is no easy matter to locate big fish in these days of overfished waters. Sometimes you meet an angler who is just boiling over with the truth, and he may honestly put you wise to a big one. But this does not happen often. However, assuming that I have found my big trout, the next consideration is a fly properly tied and suitable for his kind of water, as explained in the chapter on Hackle. Then your fly should represent the fly or food which the fish might be looking for and feeding on at the time. Above all, your flies must be lifelike and neat. The nearer your flies come to being a representation of something that is alive, something that looks like part of the trout's diet, the better your success will be.

In catching this trout, time is very important. You require no end of it, because haste is usually the downfall of the angler instead of the fish. You cannot rush a trout. He knows and sees as much as you— possibly and probably more. A trout is usually more aware than the best fisherman, and a big trout always is.

Having considered these requirements, wade in to your chosen position, if wading is necessary. Take time and avoid any disturbance, remembering that you are stalking a piece of game as wary and difficult as any pursued by man.

I always fish my fly so that it *becomes deadly* at the point where the trout is most likely to take his food, which is usually at or close to his position in the stream. I have always contended in my mind that there is a point in fishing a fly where its appeal-efficiency is low and a point where its appeal-efficiency is high. Since my flies are tied to act lifelike and look lifelike, I fish them so that the efficiency of these qualities is at its highest when it nears and arrives before the trout for his inspection. This is accomplished by allowing a gradual increase of tension caused by the water flowing against the leader, causing the fly to lift from the bottom and rise with the hackles or legs quivering after the manner of the hatching natural fly.

Imagining we are on the stream, I cast my fly up and across about fifteen feet or more above where the big trout is located, depending on the pool and stream. The fly sinks to the bottom, progressing along naturally as I follow it with my rod, allowing no slack in the line but being very careful not to pull against it and cause it to move unnaturally. The fly comes straight down to him bumpety-bump over the gravel and stones along the bottom with the current. Now watch the fly. It is almost to him, and would only have to travel about four more feet to pass right by his nose without his looking at it unless it can be made to appear alive and escaping. At this point the progress of the rod following the fly is checked, and the pressure of the water against the stationary line and leader is slowly lifting the fly. Now the fly becomes slightly efficient or animated and deadly, and the trout notices it. The hackles or legs start to work, opening and closing, and our trout is backing downstream in order to watch the fly a little more, because he is not quite persuaded as yet. Now you can see the fly become even more deadly. As more water flows against the line, the fly rises higher off the bottom and the hackle is working in every fiber. It will jump out of the water in a minute, now, and the trout is coming for it. Bang! He's got it.

Here, Pete, take the rod and show me how you

handle a big fish. If you lose him it won't matter. I've got my supper in my basket and if you lose him we know where there is a big one the next time we come back.

I do not try to impart any fancy movements to my fly with my rod but simply allow the fly to advance naturally with the current over the stones and gravel until I check its progress gently by ceasing to follow it with my rod. Then the slight tension from the water pressure flowing against my leader and line causes the fly to rise slowly, opening and shutting the hackles, giving a breathing effect such as a genuine insect would have when leaving the bottom of the stream to come to the surface. The water will do all that is necessary to make a fly deadly if it is properly tied.

Most of my trout are caught by the technique explained above if the nature of the stream permits. I often adopt other tactics, but to explain them is not the purpose of this book.

Part II

THE ART OF
FISHING
THE
FLYMPH

Vernon S. Hidy

A TREATISE ON THE DELICATE TECHNIQUE
REQUIRED TO SIMULATE THE MOVEMENTS
OF HATCHING AQUATIC INSECTS

WITH REFERENCES FROM ANGLING LITERATURE
DESCRIBING THE FRUSTRATIONS OF DRY-FLY PURISTS
WHO MAY NOW SUCCEED WITH THIS MORE
SOPHISTICATED APPROACH WHEN FISHING
FOR BROWN TROUT OR RAINBOW TROUT

SOME NEW DEFINITIONS

FLYMPH—A WINGLESS ARTIFICIAL FLY with a soft, translucent body of fur or wool which blends with the undercolor of the tying silk when wet, utilizing soft hackle fibers easily activated by the currents to give the effect of an insect alive in the water, and strategically cast diagonally upstream or across for the trout to take just below or within a few inches of the surface film.

FLYMPH FISHING is that technique which, by comparison to the "chuck-and-chance-it" use of the winged wet fly, or the hard-bodied or weighted nymph fished deep, strives to simulate the hatching nymphs of the mayfly, caddis fly, or other aquatic insects as they struggle up toward the surface or drift momentarily in or just under the surface film. In suspense, visual excitement, and pleasure, flymph fishing equals or excels dry-fly fishing because the strike is usually visible and the fly must be placed upstream from the trout with considerable accuracy and skill.

13

THE FLYMPH PHENOMENON

EXPERIENCED FLY FISHERMEN and serious readers of angling literature are all familiar with the trout-stream phenomenon called "the hatch." The two most prevalent aquatic insects, the mayfly and the caddis fly, are reaching that dramatic stage of their life cycle that brings them swimming up to the surface of the water where they take wing as flies immediately or after floating momentarily to dry their wings. The caddis fly usually swims upward quite vigorously and flies off immediately, as do certain families of the mayfly. Within a day or so the duns (so called because of the dun color of their wings) mature into spinners with glassy, transparent wings and swarm together over the river in a mating flight during which the eggs of the female are fertilized. Later the mayflies drop to the water with their glassy wings outspread in the posture of dead or dying insects.

At such times it is often no easy matter to ascertain which insect the trout *prefer* since there is often more than one type of insect available to the trout during this period of the hatch. And the trout are often selective—perferring one mayfly or one caddis fly over the others.

On such occasions great anglers such as Leisenring, Skues, and Lunn (the famous river keeper) could readily bring into play their Olympian knowledge and vast experience, much to the amazement of less-experienced anglers and to the *complete chagrin* of all dry-fly purists. For, during the early stages of the hatch when the hatching insects are swimming upward and struggling to the surface to become flies, the floating fly is often completely ignored. The breaks in the surface of the water are caused by bulging and swirling trout feeding on flymphs, those insects which I have so named because they have reached that stage of their life cycle when they ascend to the surface in order to become flies. These aquatic insects have been feeding and maturing as nymphs hidden in or near the streambed in moss, weedbeds, and silt among the pebbles, twigs, and stones.

The hour of emergence may occur at any time during the day or night. Before the insects take wing above the water, however, the trout have been surreptitiously feeding on the restless nymphs-about-to-be-born-into-flies. The emergence has been well described by John Waller Hills in his book, *River Keeper:* "No one who has not seen a big hatch can imagine what it is. It is a great event of Nature. The surface, in the eddies and stiller water, is packed solid. And no one who has seen a great hatch, every female fly of which (and they are much the more numerous) has laid its six or seven thousand eggs, will feel any anxiety about the future. But he feels considerable anxiety about the present: for amid such plenty trout get gorged, they eat only an occasional fly, and are nearly uncatchable."

In the same book Hills asks the reader: "Are you sure you can distinguish a nympher from a riser? Are you sure you can always pick out one who is devouring nymphs just on or below the surface?" These are questions the fly fisherman should consider closely.

Please keep in mind that these "nymphers" are feeding on flymphs . . . insects that are swimming free in the water, kicking and wiggling their juicy, translucent bodies which are virtually irresistible to the trout. Depending on the species of mayfly or caddis, the flymphs may rise slowly or quickly in still water, swirl in the eddies, or drift downstream with the current in faster water. In any situation they are noteworthy for several reasons: the trout can see them; they may be easy or difficult for the trout to catch depending on the "competition" of other trout and the likelihood of an insect near the surface "escaping" into the air.

Relate these considerations to the bulging stomachs of trout caught during a feast on the flymphs and we may easily understand why, when flymphs are plentiful, the trout will indulge in an orgy of slashing, furious competition. At such times they will take the fly so savagely they may snap the tippet

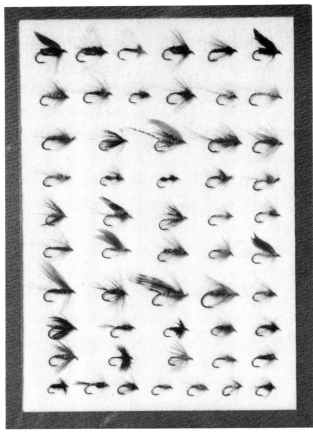

Leisenring utilized dry flies and three basic styles of wet flies, as shown in these plates of his flies in the framed collection of Pete Hidy. The three types are: Winged flies, wingless hackle flies (which Hidy prefers to designate as "flymphs") and the short-hackled thorax nymphs shown in the bottom row.

in spite of your delicate touch on the line. This possibility exists on streams holding big trout such as Oregon's Deschutes River, Idaho's Silver Creek, the Cowichan on Vancouver Island, and many of the lakes in Canada, the Pacific Northwest, and the Intermountain West.

The angler's disappointment at the loss of a big fish that he has at least deceived and felt on his line momentarily must be weighed against the possibility of not deceiving or hooking them at all. It is a hard decision the flymph fisherman must face at times: to increase your chance of deceiving and hooking a fish while decreasing your chance of holding a big fish away from the moss, weed beds, and fast water where he will inevitably break free. It is both exhilarating and unnerving to tie on progressively smaller tippets—from 3X to 4X to 5X to 6X—and reduce the size of your fly from 10 to 12 to 14 to 16 or 18 in an excited attempt to reach a combination acceptable to the big fish feeding recklessly beside or in front of you. Without an understanding of the flymph, or delicate tippets and smaller flies, you risk the frustration described by Hills in *River Keeper:*

"To see these great fish walloping about like porpoises, too intent upon their meal to take any notice of the fisherman, looking as though they could be caught by any duffer who could chuck a fly anyhow, to believe that you have before you many a splendid prize easy to be won, and then to come home with nothing, is an experience which knocks the conceit out of the most exalted."

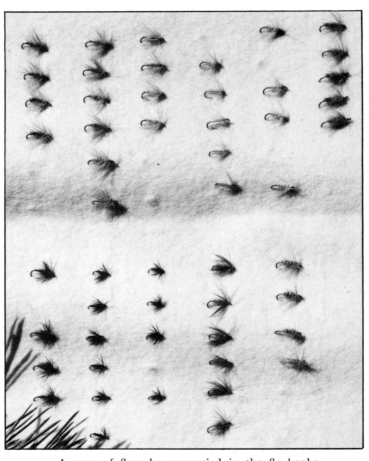

A page of flymphs, as carried in the fly books
of Jim Leisenring and Pete Hidy.

In that half-forgotten classic, *Golden Days* by Romilly Fedden, we find another interesting observation. "On this particular day the trout had been taking floating May flies for an hour past, then for no apparent reason they suddenly ceased to rise. Yet certain underwater swirls or the faint flash of a turning fish indicated that the meal was still in progress down below. Of course, the obvious deduction was that the fish were feeding on the hatching nymph before it could reach the surface."

Another incident from Hills: "I had a sharp lesson one August night from a friend, a great and ingenious angler, who was fishing with me at Stockbridge. Trout rose well: there was a noble hatch of Blue-Winged Olive; I got nothing, he got two brace. He discovered, and I did not, that trout were taking the nymph a little below the surface."

And in Negley Farson's great book, *Going Fishing,* there is this revealing comment:

"Here every evening was a rise of trout such as I would not have believed possible. You could stand on the bridge in the still spring nights and hear splash after splash. And if you waded out from the bushes at the foot of the ancient church, not caring if the water did come over your waders, you had fishing such as you might dream of in heaven. It was here that I used the unnamed fly tied by the Captain in the English Army of Occupation at Cologne. It was a whitish, hackled arrangement, with a grey body; and I fished it until there was little left of it except the bare hook. Its effectiveness increased with its bedraggled condition. Night after night I clumped back to the hotel, almost stupefied by my good luck—the miracle of that fly. And I would slide a bagful of beautiful fish out on the verandah table. In that dim porch light, with the reflection from the green vines, the beauty of those fish had something haunting about it. We loved to touch them, turn them over, pick them up, admire them. The silent shake of the old Austrian count's grey head had something reverent about it. Here was the Adoration of the Fish."

Here, then, is some of the evidence that trout prefer an emerging mayfly or caddis fly, which I prefer to identify as the flymph because it pinpoints and calls attention to the neglected drama just below the surface of the water. By comparison, the terms "wet-fly fishing" and "nymph fishing" are ambiguous and rather confusing.

Should any dry-fly purist be reluctant to share the excitement of flymph fishing, he would do well to contemplate the words of his peer, George M. L. La Branche, in *The Dry Fly and Fast Water*. In Chapter One he confesses, "the desire to take one of these fish became an obsession, and their constant rising to everything but my flies exasperated me to the point of wishing that I might bring myself to the use of dynamite."

In Chapter Three he again discusses the phenomenon of trout "feeding below the surface upon the nymphae of insects about to undergo the metamorphosis that produces the winged fly . . . and after

a succession of flies has been tried without success
the discomfited angler may be excused if he con-
cludes that his artificial is not a good imitation."
He then suggests that a hackle fly should be cast
some distance above the feeding fish "so that the
fly will approach the trout approximately as the
nymph would, i.e., under water and rising."

In a fine tribute to the delicacy and strategy
required for flymph fishing La Branche wrote: "One
fly only should be used, and quite as much care is
required in its delivery as would be necessary were
a floating fly being presented."

Some skill in the art of fishing the flymph will,
then, in the opinion of La Branche, save the angler
much exasperation and discomfiture. This neglected
technique will put him in tune with the river, the
trout, and the insect activity, increase his success,
decrease his failure, and multiply his pleasure at the
riverside.

The appreciation of flymph fishing in America
was sparked by *The Art of Tying the Wet Fly* in
1941, a time of increasing popularity for the dry fly
and great adulation for La Branche. In England,
some years earlier, F. M. Halford had, in the words
of Colonel E. W. Harding, "invested the dry fly with
such glamour and authority that there seemed almost
to be no other method worthy of the name of fly
fishing."

To counter this disproportionate emphasis, G.
E. M. Skues wrote those two English classics, *Minor
Tactics of the Chalk Stream* in 1910 and ten years

later *The Way of a Trout with a Fly.* With these books the status and prestige of "exact wet-fly fishing" were established in England. Colonel Harding described Skues's books as "the work of a man trained to reason, and of a scholar, and [the two books] will live as one of the great landmarks of fly fishing literature."

Halford and Skues in England may well be compared to La Branche and Leisenring in America. The English anglers were far more prolific in their writings, however, and they were spurred on by their rather friendly but deadly serious vendetta over the dry versus the wet fly. In contrast, their American counterparts never met and never engaged in any controversy over the merits of the techniques they advocated.

14

THE DRY FLY AND THE FLYMPH: A PARALLEL

"We fish for pleasure; I for mine, you for yours."
—LEISENRING'S *Notebooks*

THE BIG FISHING JACKET worn by Jim Leisenring has always symbolized for me the ideal range of flies required for versatility in fly fishing. The pockets contained three boxes of exquisite dry flies and two thick books of wet flies neatly arranged on felt pages bound in pigskin. He approached a stream with a strong desire to *please the trout* rather than simply gratify his personal preference for just one technique. I can still hear him say (at his fly-tying table and on the stream), "You must tie your fly and fish your fly so the trout can *enjoy* and *appreciate* it." As a result, he fished a dry fly when the trout preferred a floating fly and shifted both his techniques and his fly patterns as necessary to stay in tune with the changes in insect activity or the preferences of the trout.

His dry flies glistened with bright, stiff hackles: beautiful bivisibles, mayflies, and stone flies. The classic patterns were there: Quill Gordon, Light Cahill, Dark Cahill, Blue Dun, Pale Evening Dun, Olive Dun, and Green Drake. There were deadly-looking Black Gnats, Midges and Mosquitoes on light wire hooks as well as the Adams and March Brown. Virtually all of these could be purchased in a tackle store or ordered by mail. The wet flies in the pigskin books, however, were for sale nowhere in the world —as he tied them—and many of them had no name. "That fishes for [imitates] one of the little Sedges. This one fishes for a Dark Olive before it hatches," Leisenring would say when asked about a certain fly in his fly books.

It was readily apparent to me, as I learned his techniques, that Leisenring was having a lot more fun in his fly tying and fly fishing than most anglers, and he was catching more fish by staying in tune with the river. This basic attitude led him to a thorough study of trout-stream insects and angling literature as shown in the many notebooks he kept for his personal use and his *Color and Materials Book*. His fly books contained, therefore, an amazing range of shapes, sizes, and colors in the flies—extremely life-like there on the page dry but even more lifelike when they were wet. Once in the water they would come alive with subtle blendings of color, textures, and translucence—flashes of light from gold or silver wire ribbing, tinsel, and lively hackles. Each fly was tied to look alive when wet and act alive in the water.

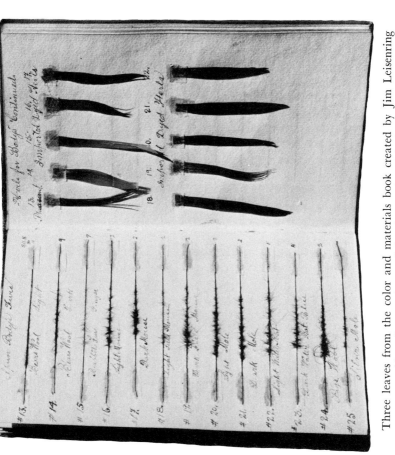

Three leaves from the color and materials book created by Jim Leisenring as a streamside reference for studying insects he wished to imitate.

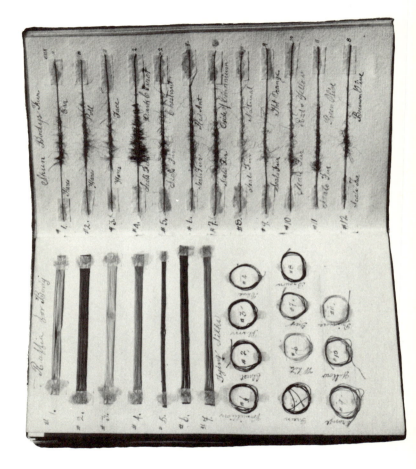

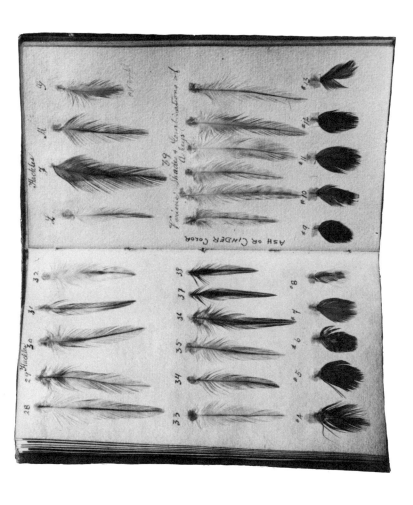

Shaders

39
Various Shades of combinations of
the ways

ASH OR CINDER COLOR

Leisenring's fly books contained a predominance of hackle flies rather than winged wet flies or short-hackled, thorax-type nymphs which are, of course, effective at times. In my experience it is the hackle fly that provides the tremendous excitement for the fisherman and the fish just below the surface of the water, and deserves, therefore, the name "flymph" to dramatize this unique appeal to trout which has been, and will continue to be, of increasing interest to those primarily concerned with the two-dimension limitations of the floating fly because they need it so very much.

To encourage dry-fly anglers to explore the excitement of the flymph I will quote two respected writers, one English and one American, and bring the rationale to a climax with some comments by Ernest Schwiebert and Art Flick, two contemporary anglers whose books are of interest to all fly fishermen.

In 1885 T. E. Pritt, a distinguished angler and the angling editor of the *Yorkshire Post,* wrote the book *Yorkshire Trout Flies* which was so warmly received by anglers that it was published again in 1886 with the title *North-Country Flies.* Both editions are collectors' items today, and they deserve to rank among the classics of angling literature. Pritt's statement regarding the "appearance of vitality" in wingless flies deserves the attention of every fly fisherman who seeks to "please" the trout and thus become a more versatile, more successful angler.

Pritt said: "It is now conceded that a fly dressed hacklewise is generally to be preferred to a winged imitation. The reasons for this are not far to seek and are satisfactory. It is far more difficult to imitate a perfect insect and to afterwards impart to it a semblance of life in or on the water, than it is to produce something which is sufficiently near a resemblance of an imperfectly developed insect, struggling to attain the surface of the stream. Trout undoubtedly take a hackled fly for the insect just rising from the pupa in a half-drowned state; and the opening and closing of the fibers of the feathers give it an appearance of vitality, which even the most dexterous fly-fisher will fail to impart to the winged imitation. Perhaps too much attention is commonly given to the wings of artificial flies, and too little to the bodies.''

This relates logically to Leisenring's comment on wings in Chapter Eight: "I could always, and still can, catch more fish on a wingless imitation." Of his twelve favorite patterns listed in Chapter Nine, eight patterns were fished by Leisenring as flymphs: the Old Blue Dun, Blue Dun Hackle, Black Gnat, Iron Blue Wingless, Light Snipe and Yellow, Pale Watery Dun Wingless, Tup's Nymph and the Iron Blue Nymph. Four other hackle flies which ranked high in his favor as shown by his comments and detailed dressings are: the Doctor Lyte Palmer, and the spiders of W. C. Stewart—the Black Spider, the Red Spider, and the Dun Spider.

John Atherton, a well-loved and respected member of the Anglers' Club of New York, made the following remarks in his brilliant book, *The Fly and the Fish,* published in 1951 and a much-sought collectors' item today.

"We are apt to neglect the wet fly when fish are rising, and when we find they do not take the dry fly well, we blame it on the pattern. It is quite possible that wet-fly fishing and dry-fly fishing shade into one another on occasion, the dividing line being indiscernible. For instance, when the trout are taking small flies in the surface film not visible to us, we may be at a loss to solve the problem. A very thin, delicate wet fly, similar to those used by Mr. Hewitt in fishing the Neversink flats late in the evening, might be a good solution. I would suggest that in tying flies of this type the less dressing the better, within reason, as the trout get a very close look at the fly in the surface film or under the surface. This is particularly true in the evening when their vision is very acute."

Ernest Schwiebert's great book, *Matching the Hatch,* appeared in 1955 to give American anglers their most complete insight into the appearance, behavior, and availability of aquatic insects month by month in the East and in some areas of the West. His lists of fly dressings include imitations of all the aquatic insects plus some terrestrial insects of importance to the fly fisherman. Schwiebert is the first angler, to my knowledge, to specify a dressing for an insect at the moment of its emergence. He specifies that a "Wet-fly subimago pattern [page 189 of the first edition] imitates the *'emerging March Brown.'*

This book provides much valuable information for fly fishermen on trout-stream entomology as seen through the eyes of an extremely versatile angler who is also a talented amateur entomologist with a rare gift of philosophical detachment in his writings and conversation.

"During the emergence [of the Green Drake] the nymphs dart quickly to the surface," Schwiebert observes. "Often the largest fish feeding are never seen at the surface. They are content to take the nymphs under water as soon as they show themselves in the dash for the surface."

Some "two-pound browns working methodically during a hatch of the Blue-Winged Olive" led Schwiebert into the usual routine of the dry-fly angler: "I caught no trout for one hour while the browns rolled steadily all around me. It was ten minutes and one two-pounder before the hatch was over that I discovered they were nymphing." For so experienced an angler as Ernest to be seduced by the dry-fly mystique as recently as 1955 is a significant commentary on the "conventional wisdom" which has kept many fly-fishermen "retarded" by comparison with the state of the art achieved by those anglers here and abroad who enjoy using the hackle-fly flymph just below the surface of the water.

The close relationship between the flymph and the dry fly is clearly revealed in Art Flick's *New Streamside Guide*, republished in 1969 after being out of print for several years. I strongly recommend

On Idaho's Silver Creek, the flymph fished on longer leaders with tippets of 5X or 6X will attract trout from the moss beds when there is no wind to ruffle the clear water—and when there is no interest in a floating fly.

this and Schwiebert's book for valuable lessons in entomology extending over many years on many trout waters. Flick will reassure you in Chapter 15, for example, that "it is a known fact that nymphs are most active just prior to the time that the fly emerges." He also points out that fishing the Hendrickson nymph prior to a hatch "has special appeal to the dry-fly fisherman for exactly the same tackle is used as for dry flies, excepting the fly, of course, and they are used at a time when dry-fly fishing is apt to be unproductive."

I have selected these few observations from the writings of other anglers to show the logic, the efficacy, and the inevitability of some new terminology such as "flymph fishing," which will be far more acceptable to the dry-fly fisherman than the terms "wet-fly fishing" or "nymph fishing." The new terminology clarifies and identifies a specific technique, opens the way for much pleasure for many previously uninformed or prejudiced anglers, and hastens the day when the two-dimensional dry fly will be viewed as one of the *two* most sophisticated and most exciting methods of fly fishing. Future anglers may well consider the three-dimensional flymph technique as *more exciting* than the dry since it requires a keener observation, greater finesse, and a more delicate touch at the fly-tying table and on the stream.

15

FISHING THE FLYMPH

THE SIMILARITY BETWEEN FISHING the dry fly and a delicate, sparsely tied flymph is very great, as indicated by the comments of La Branche, Schwiebert, and Flick. With an understanding of insect behavior and the willingness to explore the more delicate and sophisticated technique of fishing the flymph, the angler should give some thought to the use of more delicate tackle. You will find the Hardy Corona silk line extremely satisfactory. I recommend size IFI which tapers from .035 in the middle to .022 at the ends, or size HDH which tapers from .045 at the middle to .025 at the ends.

Silk lines require thorough dressing with Mucilin to keep them floating. If you dress them well they will retain their strength and pliability for ten or fifteen years or more. Remove them from the spool and hang them in loose coils for ventilation when not in use. Silk lines cast well and seem to improve through the years with careful treatment. They do not throw big shadows or spook the trout as much as the thicker synthetic lines used by most fishermen today. Two Coronas and a Hardy Princess reel with an extra spool will enable you to change lines if one becomes water-soaked and tends to sink.

The flymph can be fished, of course, with heavier and coarser lines, particularly on windy days or in fast, rough water. The ideal presentation, however, is more easily achieved with a light line. This is always essential on quiet water where, as a rule, the heavier lines will spook the fish and detract from your success and pleasure.

The lighter lines also permit more accurate short casts. Under certain conditions you may stalk a good trout and fish for it from surprisingly close in. This can be exciting and habit forming. You have the suspense of the close-up view of the trout's approach, his deliberate, twisting satisfaction in taking the fly and the tingle of your nerves in deciding when and how hard to set the fly. At such times you may care to try a maneuver or strategy explained to me by Lee Wulff.

With a minimum of tension let the fish virtually hook itself and permit it to keep moving naturally without knowing it has been hooked. You must be standing in the water and able to play the fish through the complete circle of 360 degrees. In some instances, *not always,* you will be able to submerge your net and gently guide the fish into a position for netting . . . and net him! . . . before he knows he is in trouble. I have been able to do this on two occasions when I was standing in the shade in about four feet of water and virtually invisible to the trout.

In some instances I have seen the fish eject the fly and in other instances I have lost the fish at the instant of netting. This is, however, exciting sport which can be enjoyed with a floating as well as a submerged fly.

The most desirable leaders are those that have no glare, of course, and they should be no shorter than nine feet. Leaders of twelve feet or fourteen feet should be used on extremely clear water when there is no wind to ruffle the surface. For best results you will want to use 5X tippets (one-pound test) or 6X tippets (three-quarters-pound test) although 4X and 7X may be more logical at certain times according to your mood, the size of the insects, and the currents and the fish.

One must watch for the more subtle evidences of a "take" which always occur, in flymph fishing, just below the surface of the water.

Evidences of a striking trout are, in the order of their visibility to the angler:

(1) The heavy slashing swirl of the trout which may cause an audible splash or plop when the fly is in or near the surface film.

(2) A humping of the water caused by the arching, curved ascent and descent of the trout as it rises, takes the fly, and returns to its position lower in the water.

(3) A flash or gleam beneath the surface—the silver of a rainbow or the golden yellow of the brown or cutthroat—caused by the tilt of the trout's body when it turns to take the fly.

The flymph fisherman takes care at all times to avoid slack in his line or leader. This precaution begins with the tug he gives his line after he casts. The tug straightens his leader and gives him a precise, direct control of the fly as it moves, drifting with the current naturally or curving downstream and across the feeding position of the trout, depending upon the strategy and the position of the angler.

Sensitive handling of the line by the left hand gives the flymph fisherman the advantage (over the dry-fly angler) of receiving various kinds of "messages" from his fly. The messages are extremely important when the light conditions do not permit the angler to see direct evidence of a striking trout. The messages range from the powerful strike of a big fish (that pulls the line from your fingers or through your fingers, which "brake" it and cushion the shock occurring when the fish begins to pull line from your reel), to the "tap" of smaller fish, and the "pause" which can mean several things: the slow take of a good trout, the hook or leader touching moss or weeds, or the sudden take and ejection of the fly by a fish.

The two most critical and decisive considerations in fishing the flymph are, surely, the angler's willingness to use extremely light tippets and his foresight in securing patterns of flymph flies with soft, translucent bodies of fur or wool that blend with the undercolor of the tying silk when wet, and hackle fibers that can be activated by the currents to give the effect of an insect alive in the water.

Raising your rod high will bring the flymph up toward the surface and activate the hackles of the fly as it nears the feeding position of the trout.

A tube-floater on Idaho's Silver Creek will observe many trout swirling to flymphs as they rise to the surface from the moss bed in the stream or from the silt and weedbeds near the bank.

The Kamloops trout of British Columbia find the hackle fly fished below the surface virtually irresistible, creating solid swirls when taking near the surface and flashes of silver that can often be seen as they turn to take the fly in deeper water.

The flymph may be fished directly upstream but the retrieve of the line is much easier in casting diagonally upstream or across so the flymph may swing a little in arriving at the feeding zone of a trout. In my opinion the swing of the fly activates the hackles in a manner that is extremely desirable since insects swim erratically and haphazardly enough to justify this presentation which would be called "drag" in fishing a dry fly. In quiet water without currents I occasionally twitch a flymph slightly to attract attention if the trout are inactive and, if the wind is blowing rather strongly against my line, I have found that it can be advisable to offset this by lowering and raising my rod slightly.

In his remarkable chapter "Trout Fishing With A Wet Fly," in his classic book *Fly Fishing,* Viscount Grey tried, as a diplomat serving his country in the embassies of Europe, to calm the troubled waters of controversy among British anglers at the turn of the century. His words are still relevant today. "The enthusiasm which was the result of dry-fly fishing led at one time, among those who were fortunate enough to be able to enjoy it, to a tendency to disparage the older art of using the wet fly. A comparison of the two methods is always interesting, but it must never be forgotten that it is not necessary, nor even appropriate, to exalt the one at the expense of the other. It is true that there are rivers on which the two methods overlap, and where each can be used, but even in such places it will be found that the weather, the season, or the character of the water decides from time to time in favor of one method or the other. It is the habit nowadays for nations to divide maps into what they call spheres of influence; a division which sometimes accords with geographical conditions, and at other times is arbitrary. Something of the same kind is possible between the wet fly and the dry fly, but with this advantage as applied to angling, that the division of the spheres of influence is not arbitrary, but prescribed by natural conditions, and likely to be maintained by them."

To the reasons which "decide from time to time in favor of one method or the other" I would only add the one that must be the most important reason of all: *the preference of the trout.*

I would hope that fly fishermen of all persuasions would find an acceptable middle ground in the few inches of water which I suggest are the rightful domain of the flymph—a fresh new word untainted by controversy and intended to serve only as a guide to pleasure, satisfaction, and excitement.

INDEX